SELECTED POETRY OF
ARCHIBALD LAMPMAN

SELECTED POETRY OF

ARCHIBALD LAMPMAN

EDITED AND INTRODUCED BY

MICHAEL GNAROWSKI

THE TECUMSEH PRESS OTTAWA

ISBN 0-919662-14-5 (casebound)
ISBN 0-919662-15-3 (paperback)

The Editor and Publishers gratefully acknowledge the support of the Ontario Arts Council.

Canadian Cataloguing in Publication Data

Lampman, Archibald, 1861-1899
Selected Poetry of Archibald Lampman

Bibliography: p.
ISBN 0-919662-14-5 (bound). -
ISBN 0-919662-15-3 (pbk.)

I. Gnarowski, Michael, 1934- II. Title

PS8473.A44A17 1987 C811'.4 C81-090006-8
PR9199.2.L35A17 1987

Design and layout: Robert Chitty

Dedication

Someday we shall come again to the poem
(Louis Dudek)

ACKNOWLEDGEMENTS

Many helped — directly and indirectly — in the process that was the long hatching of this little book. Carleton University, and my Deans, Naomi Griffiths and Janice Yalden, provided financial support and much encouragement. I owe, of course, an immense debt to Lampman scholars who, in many and various ways, and as colleagues, associates and friends, went before and broke trail: notably, Helen Lynn, David Bentley and Margaret Whitridge, and to all the librarians and archivists whose intelligent hoarding makes all things possible ! To Louis Dudek, teacher and friend these thirty eight years, I owe ... and owe ... and owe ...
To Glenn Clever, Frank Tierney and Bob Chitty, my thanks for giving new meaning to the word patience.

M.G.

CONTENTS

Introduction 1

The Poetry 37

from *Among the Millet* (1888)

April 39
The Frogs 42
Heat 45
Among the Timothy 47
Freedom 50
Morning on the Lievres 52
In October 54
Winter 55
Winter Hues Recalled 57
Despondency 60
Gentleness 61
The Truth 62
A Night of Storm 63
The Railway Station 64
In November 65
The City 66
Solitude 67

from *Lyrics of Earth* [1896]

April in the Hills 68
Life and Nature 70
After Rain 71
Comfort of the Fields 73
September 75
An Autumn Landscape 77
In November 79
Snowbirds 81

from *Alcyone* (1899)

Alcyone 82
The City of the End of Things 84
Personality 87
The Clearer Self 88
To the Prophetic Soul 89
The Land of Pallas 90
A Thunderstorm 95
The City 96
An Ode to the Hills 98
Indian Summer 102
Good Speech 102
We Too Shall Sleep 103

The Poems: Notes and References 104

Bibliography 113

INTRODUCTION

INTRODUCTION

Archibald Lampman was born on 17 November 1861 in the village of Morpeth, Ontario, then Canada West. On his mother's side Lampman was descended from a notable Swiss-German family, the Gesners, who had first migrated to America, and, as Loyalists, had moved to Nova Scotia. The Gesners claimed Konrad von Gesner (1516-1565) of Zurich as an ancestor. His scientific work represents one of the foundations of modern zoology. That branch of the family also produced Abraham Gesner (1797-1864) of Cornwallis, Nova Scotia, a scientist and inventor who developed kerosene and pioneered many of the distillation methods employed in the petroleum industry.

Lampman's father, also called Archibald, was a clergyman of the Church of England who was modestly established in Morpeth. After the poet's birth there followed a series of moves for the family to Perrytown and Gore's Landing on Rice Lake where the young Lampman began his schooling. In 1874 the Lampmans moved to Cobourg, and young Archibald entered the Cobourg Collegiate Institute where, as Carl Y. Connor reports it, he achieved an adequate scholastic record. In 1876 he transferred to Trinity College School in Port Hope where he began to show greater assiduity in his studies while maintaining a generally congenial set of friendships. Trinity College School was, for Lampman, a training ground before his passing as Foundation Scholar in 1879 into Trinity University in Toronto. Here Lampman quickly entered into college life and its activities. He was a good student who showed an early interest in writing, and who began to contribute to the student magazine, *Rouge et Noir*. Some of these early essays show a noteworthy interest in European (as opposed, exclusively, to British) culture and intellectual life. Thus there were essays on, "German Patriotic Poetry" and on "Leon Gambetta" (1838-1882), the French republican leader prominent in French politics in the aftermath of the Franco-Prussian War (1870-1871), an event in which, incidentally, Lampman had shown some interest. He wrote, as well, on Shelley's "Revolt of Islam" and on "Friendship" suggesting, in the latter, that the advance of civilization was making men more selfish and ruthless, a theme that would emerge as a concern in his poetry in later years. At the same time, it should be noted that Lampman's preoccupation with literary fellowship and student activities at college diverted his energies and cost him a first class degree. In 1882 he began to cast about for suitable employment. School-mastering offered itself as the likeliest prospect, and after applying for a teaching position in various small towns in Ontario, he was offered a post of Assistant Master in the High School in Orangeville. He wrote his final examinations in October while in the midst of his school work, and graduated with second class honours.

Very quickly, Lampman found teaching an uncongenial way to make his living, and his letters to friends reveal a desire to escape that life. With the help of a college friend, Archibald Campbell, whose father had been Postmaster General of Canada, Lampman secured a modest clerkship in the Post Office Department in Ottawa and, on 11 January 1883, having resigned from the school in Orangeville, he moved to Ottawa.

In Ottawa, Lampman settled into an undemanding routine at the Post Office. He would now have time to write, and appears to have been generally satisfied with his situation. Parts of a letter which he wrote at this time, and which is cited by Connor in his study of Lampman is worth quoting. He said:

"I have been dreaming a great deal lately , sitting in the evenings with my pipe between my teeth, in an armchair, Matthew [Arnold] and Swinburne at my elbow and Shelley on my knee. . . . The novel, which has become a pet scheme with me and much of the matter of which has been fermenting in my head, must be abandoned for this year any way. I am in a very good condition for verse making, as I am altogether undisturbed through the long evenings. . . . I like the Civil Service. . . . I go to work at 9.30, taking lunch with me; get away at four,have dinner at six, and do nothing the rest of the time. . . I am getting a most comfortable ease of versification nowadays from continual practice, which removes every hindrance from my way. . ."

(Connor, 67)

In spite of the generally contented tone of Lampman's letter, there is a frequently sounded counterpoint in other letters in which he expresses boredom with his job and a querulous lack of confidence in his own writing ability. Late in 1883, Lampman's family moved from Toronto to Ottawa to join him, and in December of that year he published a poem in the first issue of *The Week,* a literary periodical under the editorship of Charles G.D. Roberts, who was destined to become the leading figure of that group of Canadian writers who would be known as the Confederation Poets. They distinguished themselves not only by the strong native strain in their poetry, but also by the fact that they were the first Canadian poets who, taken as a group, had had the benefit of a serious and professional study of literature at university (except for D.C. Scott), an experience that honed their aesthetic and critical senses, and made them professionally competent and alive to the needs and dictates of their art.

In February of 1884, Lampman's idol, Matthew

Arnold came to Ottawa on his North American speaking tour.[1] Lampman was curiously subdued and circumspect about this event, although eight years later he would be planning a never-to-be-written "elaborate article on Matthew Arnold". However, writing to his friend J.A. Ritchie at the time of the visit Lampman had only this to say about the much-admired Arnold:

> "I went to hear Matthew Arnold and was filled with an abiding sense of reverence and affection for that splendid old fellow, who looks and acts and speaks as nobly as he writes. Mr. Louis Frechette has taken offense at some of his stingless words in Montreal . . ."
>
> (Connor, 76)

At the same time, Lampman was also entering upon the first full phase of his life as a poet and member of the Ottawa community. Always shy and somewhat reclusive, he began to make important friends in a small but lively circle of Ottawa intellectuals, scientists and fellow civil servants. He forged a close and invaluable friendship with Duncan Campbell Scott (1862-1947), poet, writer of short stories and distinguished public servant, and associated informally with William Dawson LeSueur (1840-1917) noted thinker and critic who became Secretary of the Post Office Department in 1888 and who was, in all likelihood, Lampman's patron and protector at work. J.H. Brown (1859-1946), also of the Post Office Department, who published *Poems, Lyrical and Dramatic* in 1892, was a contemporary in Ottawa. This circle of stimulating friends and associates also included James M. Macoun (1862-1920) a biologist with the Geological Survey of Canada and, reputedly, a strong socialist; the poet and dramatist William W. Campbell (1861-1918); and the expatriate Canadian writer E.W. Thomson (1849-1924) with whom Lampman maintained a lively correspondence.[2] Lampman belonged to the Ottawa Literary and Scientific Society[3] at the meetings of which he would, on occasion, read a poem or present a paper, and, as a dedicated naturalist, Lampman had also joined The Ottawa Field Naturalists' Club in 1884 and the Audubon Society in 1887. These friendships and associations, which had been a convivial habit and valued pastime since his days at university, helped Lampman to crystallize his own social ideals. He despised wealth; believed in the full equality of women, and described himself as a "socialist".[4]

In 1887, Lampman married Emma Maud Playter (1867-1910), the daughter of Dr. Edward Playter, an eminent physician and public health pioneer, and sometime editor and publisher of several journals relating to public health, including *Sanitary Journal,*[5] *Canadian Health Journal,* and *Man*. It was in the latter periodical that Lampman, during his courtship of Miss Playter, published his prose fairy tale "Hans Fingerhut's Frog Lesson" and the poem "An October Sunset". The Lampmans had three children,[6] a daughter Natalie (b. 1892), and two sons, Arnold (1894) and Archibald Otto (b. 1898). Arnold's death shortly after his birth had a profound effect on Lampman, and is recorded in his poem "We Too Shall Sleep".

Late in 1888, Lampman published privately his first collection of verse, *Among the Millet and Other Poems.* It bore the imprint of J. Durie and Son, an Ottawa bookseller, and although Lampman had modest expectations for the volume, referring to it in a letter of 27 December 1888 addressed to W.D. Lighthall as "my little book", and adding: "The sale of my book will be necessarily very slow and scattered . . .", *Among the Millet* was, generally, well received by the critics. Fidelis (Agnes Maule Machar, 1837-1927), a poet in her own right, and writing in *The Week,* 22 March 1889, thought that Lampman's poems exhibited ". . .a high degree of general artistic excellence and careful technique. . .", while William Dean Howells (1837-1920),[7] the distinguished American editor and man of letters, concluded his review in the influential *Harper's New Monthly Magazine* for April 1889 with the opinion that ". . .we believe that his [Lampman's] fame can only await the knowledge of work very uncommon in any time."; and even the ponderous reviewer of the London magazine *The Spectator* (12 January 1889) had to concede that " . . . Mr. Lampman is at his best in his fine pictures of the Canadian scenery."

With the publication of *Among the Millet* Lampman's standing and reputation among the poets of his generation and with a small but discriminating audience began to grow, and although he would never enjoy the fame of a Charles G.D. Roberts, or the popularity of a Bliss Carman, nor the long but steady haul to a major reputation of a Duncan Campbell Scott, he would be recognised as a master craftsman by his contemporaries.

For a first book, *Among the Millet* was a strong collection of some one hundred and fifty-one pages of varied forms and styles of verse displaying the full range of Lampman's poetic interests and preoccupations. It also demonstrated that in spite of his relative youth, Lampman was an accomplished and confident artist who had positioned himself and his sensibility in a way that would enable him to draw on the rich store of image and experience afforded by nature. He had been schooled in the great tradition of English letters, and he made no secret of his admiration for certain writers of that tradition upon which he drew in a creative and inspired fashion. But *Among the Millet* and the poems that would follow in his later writing life were clearly the product of his own thought and experience, and were offered as a refashioning of literary givens in the form of a distinctly Canadian statement.

In 1890, Lampman began his important, eight-year correspondence with fellow poet, short-story writer and kindred spirit, E.W. Thomson (1849-1924). Thomson, who was then an editorial writer for the Toronto *Globe,* would resign his position in 1891 on a matter of political principle—specifically, on the issue of trade reciprocity with the United States in which he saw the danger of annexation for Canada— and would become an expatriate Canadian working as a revising editor for a Boston magazine called *The Youth's Companion.* It would be in the pages of *The Youth's Companion* that Lampman would publish twenty-six poems, the greatest number that he placed in any single magazine in the span of his short career. It is also in this correspondence with Thomson who was a dozen years older, that we get an insight into the daily round of Lampman's life, and something of a record of his reticent and, at times, his self-deprecating nature.

The friendship owed its beginnings[8] to an editorial which Thomson had written in the *Globe* on 12 March 1890 urging that the government of the day recognise literary talent such as Lampman's and offer it preferment by way of a sinecure. Thomson's gesture was instrumental not only in firming up a literary friendship, but would lead to other things as well. It would mean a trip to Boston for Lampman in 1891 with a round of visits among its literary community and the briefly held promise of a possible teaching appointment at Cornell University in Ithaca, New York. The intermediary here was Moses Coit Tyler, Professor of History at Cornell, who, in 1892, tried to find a vacancy at that university for Lampman. In the same year, W.D. Lighthall, the Montreal author and anthologist who had included six of Lampman's poems in his influential collection, *Songs of the Great Dominion: Voices from the Forests and Waters, the Settlements and Cities of Canada* (London, 1889), alerted Lampman to a vacant lectureship in German. This Lampman declined, as he would decline in 1893 Thomson's offer of a readership on *The Youth's Companion*. These and other well-intentioned efforts by his friends on behalf of Lampman are of interest because they relate to the tone of ennui and, it is supposed, of work and Ottawa-related malaise which surfaces from time to time in Lampman's poems. Critics and literary historians have argued this point[9] at some length, although the soundest conclusion appears to be that Lampman suffered from bouts of melancholy and discontent which were probably due to his fragile health, a not particularly interesting or fulfilling job, and the poor luck he had in securing a publisher for his second and third collections of poems. It should be noted, as well, that Lampman's mature and creative life (the two overlap almost completely) covered a brief span of a dozen years. He was married in 1887; published his first collection of verse in 1888, and his second book, after much difficulty, in 1896. He was dead early in 1899, at the age of thirty-seven, and without having seen his third volume of poetry in print. The intervening years had been a time of indifferent health and emotional turmoil,[10] compounded by the death of his infant son in 1894 and of his father, Archibald Sr., in 1897.[11]

Shortly before the birth of his daughter, Lampman announced in a letter to E.W. Thomson dated 9 December 1891 that "... I hope before another year passes I may be in a position to salute my friends with another book." This was, as events would sadly prove, an overly optimistic outlook. The collection in question, *Lyrics of Earth,* would take four years of frustrating effort and several rejections before it would find its way into print.[12] In addition, the early 1890's were an irksome time for Lampman. His letters to Thomson are peppered with expressions of disaffection with the civil service and distaste for the corrupt politicians who ran the country.[13] His efforts to get a second collection of verse into print —*Lyrics of Earth*— finally succeeded through the kind offices of Thomson to whom Lampman had given a free hand in the search for a publisher and, much more important, in the arrangement of the poems in the collection. The appearance of *Lyrics of Earth* in March 1896 came almost too soon after the death of his infant son, Arnold, to be of solace or satisfaction.

The only consolation for Lampman in these years was his network of friends[14] among whom Thomson appears to have been pre-eminent. Lampman had visited his friend in Boston in August of 1891, and, during 1892, the two men had been urging one another to visit their respective cities. But the expense of moving into a large[15] house at 369 Daly Avenue had made travel unaffordable for Lampman, and he had written Thomson on 20 October 1892 to this effect:

> "As to your so kind invitation to visit you, the idea of going either to New York or Boston this winter had passed completely out of my mind. My big house will make me pay for my room & comfort in increased expense for fuel & rent."
> (Lynn, 53)

In February of that year, Lampman had joined forces with Duncan Campbell Scott and William Wilfred Campbell — an individual whom Lampman had described to Thomson in a letter of 16 February 1892 as an "odd fish" and as "deplorably poor" — to write a column for the Toronto *Globe.* This intellectual enterprise which lasted from 6 February 1892 to 1 July 1893 was conceived by Lampman and Scott as a means to supplement Campbell's income. It was called "At the Mermaid Inn", appeared every Saturday with one exception, and earned the contributors three dollars a week. Lampman, who figures as the most prolific contributor, penned eighty-seven entries which constitute a fascinating record of his interests, ideas and opinions, albeit telescoped into a rather limited period of time. Characteristic of Lampman's eclectic approach in "At the Mermaid Inn" are the contributions which he wrote in the last month of the column's existence. He managed to work in praise of a poem by his friend Thomson and of the latter's employer, *The Youth's Companion,* which had always proved so hospitable to his own poems; to exercise his social conscience by rejecting the inequalities imposed on servants by their employers, " ...no one has a right at the present day to treat another openly as a social inferior ..."; and to display his naturalist's predispositions by praising the establishment of a national park in Banff, and by condemning the "...awful destructiveness of the human race ..." manifested, according to the poet, in the disappearance of the pine forests, the buffalo, and the wild pigeon.

In the Spring of 1893, a year marked by financial recession, political turmoil, heated debate about trade reciprocity with the United States, fears of annexation, and the welling up of strong temperance feelings in Canada, Lampman travelled in April to visit Thomson in Boston. Earlier, in February, Lampman had gently set aside as an impractical[16] alternative, Thomson's offer to secure for him a readership on *The Youth's Companion,* and had begged off Thomson's urgings that he establish the right connections among the powerful of Ottawa by calling on Mrs. J.N. Kirchhoffer,[17] wife of a Senator, and a "dear and brilliant friend" of Thomson's who, the latter believed, "will have more influence in two years from now than any man in Ottawa". It was not to be, and while Lampman pleaded shyness, this was in marked contrast to the comfortable socialising at which he had proved so capable during his visit to Boston two years earlier.

1893 was also the year of the Chicago Columbian Exposition, an event at which Canada is said to have exhibited with conspicuous success, and one that Lampman would have dearly liked to attend. Instead, he had to content himself with writing a poem[18] and having a presentation photograph of himself taken by an Ottawa photographer with the Exposition symbol embossed on its mat. At the same time, Lampman's frustration at his lack of success in placing a manuscript with a publisher grew apace. In 1891, during his visit to Boston, Lampman had made many valuable contacts and friendships among that city's circle of publishers, editors and literati. Horace E. Scudder, editor of the *Atlantic Monthly* was one of the individuals in whose interest and patronage Lampman put much stock, and while the *Atlantic* took Lampman's poems regularly, this prestigious connection did not seem to have a persuasive effect with Houghton Mifflin & Co. whom Lampman approached with several differently conceived and arranged manuscripts. As a matter of fact, Lampman had put on a rare effort in self promotion and literary salesmanship between

1891 and 1895 when, after having tried four publishers, it became finally possible for him to place *Lyrics of Earth* with Copeland and Day — and that through the good offices of his friend Thomson. The publication of his second collection of verse must have been a mixed blessing for Lampman. It is true that a good deal of effort had finally been rewarded by the appearance of a book. But it was a spare collection, a small volume of some fifty pages, and not quite to his liking as far as the arrangement of its poems was concerned. *Lyrics of Earth* took forever to appear, and when it did come out, it received scant attention from the critics. This must have been particularly galling to Lampman who — modesty notwithstanding — knew that he had an established reputation and something of a following in the literary world of his day.

With the official[19] release in March of 1896 of *Lyrics of Earth,* Lampman, then a little more than thirty-four years of age, entered upon the last phase of his career. He had a scant three years to live. His mental well-being became a matter of some preoccupation,[20] and although he remained physically active and full of plans for the future, his life was winding to its tragically early close.

On the 23rd of June of that year, Wilfrid Laurier, after manoeuvring deftly through the political shoals of the educational rights of Manitoba's Catholic (and essentially francophone) minority, won the general election and was set to become Prime Minister of Canada. Two days later Lampman wrote to Thomson:

> "We have had a great election here, and your old enemies are victorious all along the line.
> . . . Mr. Laurier certainly ought to be satisfied for he is the great hero of the hour from one end of the Dominion to the other."
>
> (Lynn, 173)

In the same letter, Lampman wondered about the fate of his collection of sonnets which had been offered to Copeland & Day. His tone, as far as his work was concerned was becoming more pessimistic, and he showed an inclination to think less of himself as a poet. In his letter to Thomson of 20 July 1896 Lampman sent on what was probably an early version of the manuscript of *Alcyone* which he wanted Thomson to transmit to Copeland & Day. Of himself he wrote:

> "I shall do no more work for some time. I have very little time or solitude, and I do not feel in the humour for it. God knows what will be the result of me. I think I am less clear than ever on that point."
>
> (Lynn, 175)

A few days later he was off on a major canoe trip with his brothers-in-law into Northern Ontario. He returned tanned and much the better spiritually for the experience, but the physical exertions of this expedition would declare themselves before too long. Early that October Lampman wrote Thomson to thank him for his efforts in trying to place his manuscript, and informed his friend that he had just moved to a new house. This was at 187 Bay Street, and would be Lampman's last residence. These were also the months during which Lampman nursed his father through the final stages of his illness. He continued to write, and a short while after his father's death in March of 1897, Lampman rented his house, moved his family to the country outside Ottawa, and readied himself for a mid-summer junket to Nova Scotia. But the melancholy and self-doubt continued to nag at him. On 12 May 1897 he had sent Thomson his oft-quoted lines of self-appraisal:

"You overrated me. There never was any great poet, but simply a rather superior minor one, who sometimes hits upon a thing which comes uncommonly near to being very excellent."

(Lynn, 184)

On 24 June 1897, The Royal Society of Canada, to which Lampman had been elected two years earlier, commemorated the four hundredth anniversary of the visit to North America of the Italian navigator and explorer, John Cabot, by holding its annual meetings in Halifax. Lampman had described the Society's plans rather ruefully in the same letter to Thomson:

"The Royal Society are going down to Halifax in June to found a memorial of some kind to a gentleman named Cabot who is said to have discovered this country. The railway fare will be put low, and there will be much hospitality extended to the Society, of which august body even I am a member."

(Lynn, 184)

As a matter of fact, Lampman was beginning to bask in the warm glow of reputation and standing in the intellectual community. On 19 May 1897 he reported to Maud who was living in the country that:

"I have also received a huge card inviting us to a 'State Reception' — Queen's Birthday — Government House — 10 P.M. to 12 P.M. How about that ?"

(Sommers, 115)

A month later, during the visit to Halifax, Lampman would be writing Maud in some detail about the outings and entertainment laid on by the prominent citizens of that city — which included lunch with the Archibishop and a reception at the Lieutenant Governor's — for the distinguished visitor-members of the Royal Society on that Jubilee occasion.[21] Lampman appears to have benefitted from his trip. He returned in good spirits, and in July was busy mastering the art of riding a bicycle and planning a canoe trip with Duncan Campbell Scott, upon which they embarked on the last day of August. From Lampman's account of the trip in his letter to Thomson whom he had tried to entice to join the expedition, it had been, yet again, an exhilarating but strenuous undertaking.

Towards the end of the year, Lampman had become reconciled to the fact that he would not be successful in placing his latest manuscript with a publisher, and indicated to Thomson that he would be making his own arrangements for the printing of his book. In December, he entertained a visit from Hamlin Garland (1860-1940), the American novelist and supporter of the Populist party and the single tax doctrine, who had expressed admiration for Lampman's poetry, and with whom Lampman corresponded. The end of that month saw poems on their way to *The Youth's Companion,* and plans firming up for the printing of *Alcyone* in Edinburgh.

1898 opened badly for Lampman. He spent January in bed with what was clearly the advent of a serious illness of the heart, and when he finally managed to get a letter off to Thomson, he indicated that he was on an extended three-month leave from his work for reasons of health. By the end of March, Lampman reported that his leave had been extended by another three months, and he had had to put off his plans for *Alcyone* to the fall. But by the time that April had rolled around, Lampman felt sufficiently improved to broach the possibility of a visit to Boston. On the sixth of April, William Dawson LeSueur, Lampman's friend and associate at the Post Office, had written William D. Lighthall[22] in Montreal to tell the latter that Lampman's friends were trying to raise a fund of two hundred and fifty dollars in order to enable the poet to comply with his doctor's prescription to take an extended holiday at a healthy retreat where he could enjoy peace and quiet and have "...the best chance .. of partial recovery". LeSueur described Lampman's condition as ". . . heart disease in, I regret to say, a dangerously advanced form." On the twenty-first of June, the Lampman's second son, Archibald Otto was born, and, in the latter half of July, Lampman set out on an extended journey which took him, first for a stay of a couple of weeks with his friends in Montreal, a group that included the poet William Henry Drummond (1854-1907), the sculptor and pioneer in medicine R. Tait McKenzie (1867-1938), and the physician and author Andrew Macphail (1864-1938). Lampman then travelled on, taking in a brief visit to Tadoussac, a restful stay at the St. Maurice Club on Lake Wayagamack, a delightful sojourn with relatives in Nova Scotia, and a bit of a detour to visit Thomson in Boston. He had also managed, on his outward journey, to drop in on F.G. Scott (1861-1944), clergyman and poet, who lived near Quebec City. He returned home some time around the tenth of October, after an absence of almost three months and feeling somewhat guilty towards his family. He went back to the office on the fifteenth of the month apparently ". . .ever so much better and stronger . . .". At the end of November he seemed to be holding his own, reading, not writing much, completing the arrangements for the publication of what would be his last book. On the fourteenth of November, Lampman had placed an order for five hundred copies of *Alcyone* with his printers in Edinburgh. The order had been accompanied by a bank draft for thirty-three pounds and eighteen shillings, a not inconsiderable sum for the poet since it represented approximately one hundred and seventy dollars or Lampman's salary for a month and a half.

What little we know of the last weeks of Lampman's life in those early days of 1899 we owe to C.Y. Connor who describes the poet as spiritually becalmed. Toward the end of January, Lampman had an attack of the grippe which is to say a severe cold, something that he had been prone to most of his life. In this instance the cold turned into acute pneumonia, and for Lampman, with his seriously debilitated heart, the illness proved fatal. He died at one o'clock in the morning of the tenth of February. Perhaps the most moving account of his passing is contained in a letter which William W. Campbell wrote to William D. Lighthall a week later. It reads:

> "This is a terribly sad business, this, about poor Lampman. I would have written to you before, but I have, to tell the truth, been half benumbed by the shock of his death. It came very suddenly. The Saturday before we had all met at Mr[s?] Frechette's literary evening. He seemed in good spirits; though then he told me that the heart affliction was affecting his mind. So, perhaps after all it was for the best that he should be taken before his powers had waned. Life and its petty pains & squabbles dwarf into nothing in the face of such a loss to us all. The saddest thing of all is the position in which his poor wife is left. I hope the government will grant her a small pension."[23]

Duncan Campbell Scott moved quickly to aid Lampman's bereaved family. On the thirteenth of February he had cabled the printers in Edinburgh to stop work on *Alcyone.* They complied with his instructions refunding twenty-two pounds and nineteen shillings to Maud Lampman and making up a dozen copies of the book in paper covers as a gift of condolence to the family. They also expressed the hope that they would be considered for the job of printing the collected poems upon which Scott was already embarked as a measure to relieve the financial plight of Mrs. Lampman and her two children. Scott was eminently successful in his efforts, and when the collected *Poems* appeared in 1900, the volume closed with a note of appreciation signed by S.E. Dawson, W.D. LeSueur and D.C. Scott thanking all who had given of their time, work and effort as well as"... those who contributed by their subscriptions to the total amount realized for the family of the author."

For many critics and literary historians Lampman's foreshortened life became a symbol of everything that was disappointing or tragically unfulfilled in his career as a poet. But the truth of his writing life lies closer to the perception offered by his long-time friend and fellow-poet, Duncan Campbell Scott who, in an important and revealing letter to a latter day kindred spirit, the poet and anthologist Ralph Gustafson, had this to say of his erstwhile friend:

> "Lampman never wanted to be a man of affairs or felt sense at failure to be such. Actually he took a keen interest in human psychology and conduct. Some of his best poems deal with mind and possibilities of man such as "The Largest Life", "Stoic and Hedonist," etc. He was interested in both life and nature and there was no "confusion" or

"contradiction" in this. As an artist he excelled in nature work in which he had few peers: he wrote well of "life" too but no better than many others; therefore, his high place in our letters is reared on his nature poems rather than on those dealing with human affairs.

...

The cast of Lampman's nature was not towards melancholy. Like most brilliant men he had his emotional storms and variations of mood, and he had to contend with bad health which depresses anybody. He had a great sense of humor and was a man of geniality and sociability .... I cannot agree that Lampman was "cheated out of life"; that phrase is not appropriate to a man whose life was so full of endeavour and accomplishment ... What the future held for him who can predict ? All speculation is idle but one will indulge it. He was thirty-eight when he died not worn out by a conflict with Ottawa and its parochial society, but from a gradual heart-weakening and a final burst of exertion too great."

(Gnarowski, 156-157)

Scott's emphasis upon Lampman's achievement as a poet of nature is characteristic of the opinion held by almost all of the poet's friends, critics and reviewers. From the earliest notices by Howells and Thomson, to the appraisals of contemporary critics, Lampman is valued as a poet acutely sensitive to, and making successful use of, the moods and nuances of nature and the states of mind and soul which it induced in him. More accomplished at the shorter poem and the finely-wrought lyric, Lampman strove at various times to write a truly successful long poem. Some of these attempts met with criticism from Thomson, or Lampman himself found them wanting, and they were either set aside or abandoned altogether, although he did include "The Monk" and "An Athenian Reverie", two fifteen-page poems in his first collection, and "Vivia Perpetua", a poem of sixteen pages in Alcyone. Two of Lampman's longest compositions, "David and Abigail: A Poem Dialogue" and "The Story of an Affinity" were incorporated into the collected Poems by Duncan Campbell Scott after Lampman's death.

In his landscape poems, and at these he was best, Lampman is full of sharp images that take both Nature and the reader by surprise. There is a constant tussle going on in that landscape, with the seasons shouldering one another out of the way; the ploughman turning the quietly fallow sod; the streams washing and eroding their beds; the snow blanketing all things, only to be undone by the cheerful bluster of spring. The imagination is generous, the vision subtle and accurate, the phrasing always superbly apt. Lines like,

> "October with the rain of ruined leaves"
> ("September")

or,

> "A ploughman urges his dull team,
> A stooped grey figure with prone brow
> That plunges bending to the plough
> With strong, uneven steps."
> ("An Autumn Landscape")

suggest that Lampman knew exactly what the true cycle of birth, life and ultimate, unavoidable decay really meant. There is much of this idea underlying individual poems as well as the larger cycles of his collections of verse. The metaphysics of existence were never out of mind or out of sight; the pleasures of nature were never rendered paltry by sentiment.

If there is a striking and recurring preoccupation in Lampman's poems, it is that of the poet as private individual caught in a fragment of time, musing about the nature of his experience or contemplating the drift of things around him. It is as if Lampman sought to create a dreamer's island around which public events could swirl leaving the dreamer untouched. Although we cannot be sure about the nature of Lampman's dream experiences, the revealed state of his dream consciousness suggests that there is no real division between the state of being awake and that of being asleep and that, therefore, life is continuous and, consequently, one's awareness of experience is doubled or intensified. The dream state must envelop our waking moments so that there is a fusing of the waking and the dreaming state, the conscious with the unconscious, until experience becomes an uninterrupted continuum of thought and action, art and life, the real and the imagined. How much did Lampman intuit about the true nature of perception ,and what about true perception, and how much does it have to do with the poet's famous and near hallucinatory affirmation ?

"In the full furnace of this hour
My thoughts grow keen and clear"
("Heat")

The times were full of the ideas of the new psychologists, and scientists and thinking individuals were much intrigued by the notions of consciousness then being explored and expounded. Consciousness, memory and the dream state as a way of unlocking the real and the present engaged Lampman's creative process as well. But memory is a factor of things past, and here Lampman was driven into the corner of choice. He chose to range the past against the present, and from this tension he developed his major commentaries on the historicity of human experience — the poems, "The City of the End of Things" and "The Land of Pallas". The past for Lampman was peace, beauty, freedom and a meaningful life. The present was contaminated by greed and corruption and an attendant loneliness of the human spirit. This equation, though, was not without its difficulties, and, in a sense, Lampman was at odds with himself about the value and significance of the past, so much so that he sent out seemingly conflicting signals. Certainly, the past from which "The City of the End of Things" had evolved had had its glorious historical moment. That City, now ruled by a fallen idol, had once been the creation of human genius. However, the past which prefigures the somewhat arcadian present of the Land of Pallas, is a past in which men had little control over the social forces that directed them. It is a past in which they were creatures of ancient institutions that had circumscribed their personal freedom and limited their sense of autonomy.

It must be remembered that Lampman was living in a period of considerable and dramatic change. Canada (as much as any other country) was becoming a centralized political entity in which people were beginning to congregate in the cities, where government, more and more, expressed itself through its bureaucracy, and where major breakthroughs[24] in science and technology were becoming, rapidly, the stuff of everyday life. The wireless, the telephone and the railway organized life on a tighter schedule, making short shrift of distance, and destroying the peaceable quaintness and sturdy isolation of rural life. Time and time again we find Lampman drifting off into the private places of the poem and the mind as if to escape the tension between the psychological squalor of city life and the monopolistic character of government and its bureaucracy on the one hand, and the subtle needs of privacy and the freedom to ruminate on the other. In this contest of opposing imperatives, Nature became the counter energizer helping Lampman to beat off the homogenizing and collectivizing forces of a world from which he found himself to be increasingly alienated.

And yet, Lampman was very much a creature of his own times, and evidence of this is offered in many indirect ways. The 1890's were a decade of an accelerating pace of life propelled by a variety of technological advances. The Chicago Exposition of 1893 which Lampman had dearly wished to attend was an event hallmarked by its emphasis on the achjevements of science and the newly unleashed power of technology. Advances in the use of electricity, the early automobile, the telephone and various other clever devices, engines and machines overawed the thoughtful visitor, and were widely reported and discussed in the Press . In what was clearly the age of locomotion and power, Lampman's contribution was the anxious note sounded in poems like "The Railway Station", in which the image of the train embodies not only the impression of sovereign power, but carries with it the implications of loneliness, noise and separation endemic in the new technological metropolis. And while the world was dazzled by science and machinery and technological exploits to which there seemed to be no end, there were those, and Lampman was of this persuasion, who began to see the future as composed of soulless cities ruled by degenerate technocracies. It is significant that for Lampman it is the urban, which is to say the city, that threatens to become the centre of a depraved progress. In this he seems to echo the evolutionary pessimism of T.H. Huxley[25], and much more probably, Huxley's widely read and extremely popular disciple, H.G. Wells.

In spite of all of this, the struggle with the longer poems, the seeming reverses endured at the hands of disinterested publishers, the disaffection he felt for much of contemporary life, as well as Lampman's own excessively modest self-appraisal, critical opinion has placed him in the front rank of Canadian poetry, and first among the writers of the nineteenth century. In doing this it has sided unequivocally with Thomson who wrote in 1893:

> " I read yours last night with almost a new joy — the exquisite inevitableness of the words — the absolute quality of the work — the perfection, the greatness of the moods and the art, never more impressed me."
>
> (Lynn, 84)

A NOTE ON THE TEXT

The poems in this selection draw their imprimatur from the three collections published and overseen by Lampman in his lifetime. The major task, that of a complete scholarly edition of his work, remains unrealized ninety years after his death. The nearest thing to it, Duncan Campbell Scott's edition of the *Poems* (1900) was reprinted in 1974 incorporating *At the Long Sault* (1943), but it was allowed to go out of print.

In preparing these poems for publication I have retained the spelling and punctuation employed by Lampman in the original editions although, on rare occasions, I have intervened silently in order to standardize the spelling of certain recurring words such as the word "gray". In similar fashion, and this rarely, I have intervened to correct errors in spelling and sense in quoted segments of correspondence.

Difficult and obscure words are tagged with an asterisk, and a definition or explanation is supplied under the title of the poem in the "Notes and References" section at the end. The latter, in addition to supplying meanings and definitions, is also intended to point the reader — albeit selectively — to brief opinions or ampler discussions of individual poems.

Michael Gnarowski
10 February 1989

ENDNOTES TO THE INTRODUCTION

[1] Matthew Arnold (1822-1888), was a great cultural eminence in the English-speaking world in the second half of the nineteenth century. Poet, Inspector of Schools, and something of a cultural philosopher, he was much admired and keenly listened to on both sides of the Atlantic. Lampman thought highly of him and, in a sense and broadly speaking, one suspects that he tried to model his own activities on those of the great English man of letters. For example, Arnold had written essays on, " On the Modern Element in Literature" (1857); "The Study of Poetry" (1880); "John Keats" (1880); "Byron" (1881); and "Shelley" (1888), to name only a few in what was a very large output; Lampman, in his own turn, and in what suggests itself as a parallel process, had written on, "The Modern School of Poetry in England" (1885); `"Poetic Interpretation"; "The Character and Poetry of Keats" (1893); "The Poetry of Byron"; "The Revolt of Islam" (1880). In 1887, Arnold wrote an essay on the Swiss critic Henri Frédéric Amiel (1821-1881) whose *Journal Intime,* translated in 1883 and remarkable as a document of scrupulous self-observation, aroused great interest in its time. Lampman is returning what was probably a borrowed copy of the *Journal* to Thomson in 1890 (Lynn, 3). And finally, Lampman tried his hand, albeit modestly, at public lecturing, an occasional activity at which Arnold was infinitely more successful, and one that brought him, in the fall of 1883 on a grand -- some seventy speaking engagements -- lecture tour of America.

In February of 1884, Arnold visited four Canadian cities: Toronto, Ottawa, Montreal and Quebec. On the sixteenth of that month (Bruce Nesbitt has mistakenly given 1883 as the date of Arnold's lecture in Ottawa in his "Matthew Arnold in Canada: A Dialogue Begun ?" *Culture* 28: 53-54 March 1967), in Ottawa, where Lampman was in the audience which included the Governor-General, Arnold delivered his lecture "Numbers" which would cause such a furor three days later in Montreal -- obliquely alluded to by Lampman in his letter to Ritchie.

The Ottawa *Daily Citizen* reported on 18 February 1884 that the audience had been "not a very large one"; that the Governor-General and the Marchioness of Lansdowne had been present (they had invited Arnold to stay with them); that Arnold showed a "traditional English lisp and hesitancy of utterance"; and that the gist of his message had to do with "the true doctrine of the unsoundness of the majority".

"Numbers; or The Majority and the Remnant" had been written for Arnold's American lecture tour, and was delivered, reportedly, eighteen times in the United States and Canada. The lecture, which strikes one today more as a lay sermon, and for which we have what is clearly the American version of the text, is almost divided within itself in its intellectual thrust. Its opening argument, thumpingly moralistic, reminiscent of the pulpit and not loathe to invoke Plato or Isaiah when needed, attempts to call forth a dedicated "remnant" of new leaders to act against the tyranny of the mass or "numbers" in a democracy. But then Arnold's argument slides into a subtle criticism of the Roman Catholic Church and a direct attack on contemporary French culture with its "gallo-latin" traits of which "lubricity" appears to be the chief fault. The lecture ends with praise for the Anglo-Saxon peoples, and especially for America sprung from "...excellent Germanic stock, having passed through this excellent Puritan discipline . . ." which Arnold sees as " an incomparable, all-transforming remnant" to which he happily consigns the leadership of the world. Members of the French-Canadian elite who attended the lecture in Montreal felt tarred with the brush of lubricity and walked out of the hall in protest.

[2] There are two major bodies of Lampman letters that shed invaluable light on his life and the workings of his mind. The first of these is the annotated edition of the surviving letters exchanged by Lampman and Thomson in the years 1890 to 1898, edited by Helen Lynn and published in 1980. One of the interesting features of this edition is that one has the other side of the exchange ready to hand; the other body of letters is the edition of Lampman's letters, addressed mainly to his wife as well as some family correspondence and related papers, which was prepared as a Master's thesis in 1979 at Simon Fraser University by Carol Marie Sommers. It gives us some insight into Lampman's more private thoughts and moments.

[3] Stemming from the amalgamation of the Ottawa Mechanics' Institute and Athenaeum (founded as The Mechanics' Institute in 1847) and the Natural History Society of Ottawa (founded in 1863), the Ottawa Literary and Scientific Society was incorporated in 1869 and disbanded in 1907. Its offices were at 25 Sparks Street, close by the building where Lampman worked.

[4] These remarks notwithstanding, there is a paradox in Lampman's self-confessed adherence to a socialist outlook. He is most explicit in the statement of these beliefs in an undated fragment of an essay or lecture he prepared and which was published with a brief introduction by Barrie Davies first as "A Lampman Manuscript" in *Journal of Canadian Fiction* 1:2:55-58 Spring 1972, and later as "Untitled Essay on Socialism" in Barrie

Davies, ed., *Archibald Lampman: Selected Prose* (1975) pp. 51-54.

[5] Dr. Playter published his journal under several names: as *Sanitary Journal* from 1874 to 1880 and again in 1883; as *Dominion Sanitary* Journal from 1883 to 1885, and as *Man* from 1885 to 1886. Lampman's fairytale "Hans Fingerhut's Frog Lesson" first appeared in *Man* (November 1885).

[6] Natalie Lampman, the poet's first-born child and one whom he knew briefly and upon whom he doted, later married Thomas Loftus MacInnes, the son of the poet Tom MacInnes (1867-1951), probably best remembered for his *Rhymes of a Rounder* (1913) and his *Complete Poems* which were published in 1923. The Lampmans' second child, Arnold died not long after birth. The poet's second son, Archibald Otto, born eight months before Lampman's death, graduated from the Royal Military College and served with distinction in France during the First World War. He became a well-known journalist and contributor to magazines in Canada and the United States. He died in 1938.

[7] For an interesting and detailed discussion of the rival claims of Howells and Thomson as to who first "noticed" Lampman's *Among the Millet* see Eric Ball "E.W. Thomson's Review of *Among the Millet* " *Canadian Poetry: Studies, Documents and Reviews* 20:90-99 Spring/Summer 1987.

[8] See Lynn, 214-215.

[9] See Ralph Gustafson "Among the Millet" in Gna-

rowski, 142-153; and "Life and Nature: Some Re-Appraisals of Archibald Lampman" in McMullen, 1-16.

[10] For a discussion of a possible reason for Lampman's turmoil see the "Introduction" by M.C. Whitridge to *Lampman's Kate, Late Love Poems of Archibald Lampman 1887-1897*. Ottawa: Borealis Press, 1975.

[11] Two chatty letters from Lampman's father to the poet dated 30 August 1886 and 27 July 1887 survive in the Carol Sommers edition of Lampman's family correspondence. The elder Lampman, Archibald Sr. (1822-1897), a clergyman of the Anglican Church, appears to have been a bit of a sportsman who liked the outdoors and recreational fishing. Towards the end of his life, afflicted with cancer, he lived out his days with the poet's family. Lampman described the situation thus in his letter of 25 June 1896: "My father is ill, gradually succumbing to a cancerous disease which is eating away his life, and I have taken him under my own charge and am endeavouring to make things as endurable for him as possible." (Lynn, 173)

[12] For a detailed discussion of the trials and tribulations attendant upon the publication of *Lyrics of Earth,* see D.M.R. Bentley's "Introduction" in his edition of this work. See also, Peter E. Greig, ed., "A Check List of Lampman Material in the Douglas Library Archives" *Douglas Library Notes* 16:1 12-27 Autumn 1967, this being the correspondence between Lampman and H.E. Scudder and Copeland and Day about *Lyrics of Earth.*

[13] Lampman's most overt statement of criticism

about corrupt and cynical government occurs in his letter to Thomson written on 15 December 1891. It reads: "I must try however to get out of the service if possible before very long. Our pure and enlightened government are just now zealously engaged in extracting the mote out of the eye of the Civil Service, regardless of the sawlog which is in their own eye. They have prohibited the franking of letters from the 1st of January; they propose to lengthen the office hours, to forbid men going home to lunch at noon; they have instituted absurd & troublesome regulations in regard to obtaining leave of absence. In fact they are removing from the Service the only features of it which were an attraction to a man like me. All this of course in order to gull the country into an idea that they are reforming abuses & putting a stop to corrupt practices. I would like to see them smashed ! I wish I had some knowledge of political history, and some practice in writing about politics. It would be a delightful thing to have a hand in smashing them. They are a miserable set of rascals." (Lynn, 29)

The "sawlog" to which Lampman refers was the scandal surrounding Sir Hector Langevin, Minister of Public Works and certain of his friends and associates, and having to do with the granting of contracts in connection with Quebec harbour improvements. Langevin was accused of leaking information to the benefit of private contractors, with the result that the Government was defrauded of large sums of money. The scandal shook the recently re-elected (with a greatly reduced majority) administration of Sir John A. Macdonald who died on the sixth of June of that year.

Some time later, on 10 February 1893, Lampman had written Thomson in a similar frame of mind about the political scene. He said: "No sooner has the weather moderated than we have that other worse disaster the assembly of the great national dunghill or Dominion cess-pool, everything connected with which gives me sensations of unutterable loathing and horror." (Lynn, 58)

[14] In spite of a natural shyness, Lampman appears to have made friends easily and to have kept in touch with them by means of casual letters. In addition to his circle of good and close friends in the Ottawa intellectual community, he made some permanent friendships among Boston's literary circle-- J.E. Chamberlin (1851-1935), reviewer and literary journalist; Bradford Torrey (1843-1912) editor and naturalist; and Horace E. Scudder (1838-1902), editor and critic -- to which he was introduced by Thomson during the course of his first visit to that city.

Similarly, he struck up and maintained friendly relations with Montreal's *literati,* a group that included the anthologist W.D. Lighthall (1857-1954), the novelist William McLennan (1856-1904), and the dialect poet William Henry Drummond (1854-1907).

[15] In spite of his socialist leanings and his populist outlook, Lampman remained firmly middle class in his inclinations and sensibility. In his letters he grumbled about servants while remaining curiously silent about the plight of the workingman and his pitiful wages, and the fact that Ottawa was racked by unemployment and the occasional bitter and entirely justified strike. Outside of government service, Ottawa was a city of seasonal employment due to the cyclical nature of lumbering and construction. As a result, employers were likely to cut people and wages in winter, and in times of economic depression layoffs

were prolonged. As the historian J.H. Taylor writing about the Ottawa of the late 1870's and the early 1880 has put it in his, *Ottawa: An Illustrated History*, 1986, "At least one quarter of Ottawa's population would have been . . . at the edge of starvation in winter and depression; and tied to the twelve-hour days of the wage-earner when employed."

In his residential choices, too, Lampman was solidly middle class. The big new house on Daly Avenue that he mentions to Thomson was located in Sandy Hill, a newly developing and well-to-do part of Ottawa. As Taylor has it: "Those in higher income brackets were to be mostly found in Sandy Hill . . ." (84), and when the Lampmans bought their house at 187 Bay Street, they were relocating to what was, again in Taylor's words, ". . . a neighbourhood of elegant middle-class homes developed in the area of Queen Street and Bronson Avenue at the western end of Upper Town . . ." ([98]).

[16] On 21 February 1893, Lampman had responded to Thomson's offer to secure a position for him as a reader on *The Youth's Companion* in the following words: "Your letter has put me into considerable perplexity, and I have taken a few days to think about it. I feel strongly tempted, but there are several things I have to take into account, if I propose to go to Boston. You know me well enough to realize what a hapless person I am: how incapable of pushing my way among men. It is not that I am indolent; but I am constitutionally sensitive to a morbid degree. I am a great coward when it comes to taking hold of practical affairs. Then I have my wife and little child, and I do not wish to risk putting them through any experience of severe poverty. If I were alone I would not answer you by letter, but in person. I would cut the service at once & with joy." (Lynn, 65)

It should be added that, modesty notwithstanding, Lampman had a practical sense about him. In turning down the chance to move to Boston he must have remembered his letter to Maud written on 8 September 1891 during his first visit to that city. It read in part: "Boston is in most respects a frightfully expensive place to live in, but some things are cheap. I bought a pair of collars this morning for twenty five cents. Fruit is rather cheap, and furniture is cheap, but clothing and food are dear, very dear, and rent is damnable." (Sommers, 88-89)

[17] *née* Clara Howard of Guelph, Ontario, second wife of the Hon. John Nesbitt Kirchhoffer (1848-1914) who was called to the Senate in 1892 by the Earl of Derby.

[18] "To Chicago" collected in *Lampman's Sonnets [:] 1884-1899*. Edited and introduced by Margaret Coulby Whitridge (Ottawa: Borealis Press, 1976) p.118.

[19] Although the title page of the book suggests that *Lyrics of Earth* was "published" in 1895, and although the printer's declaration states that it was actually printed in March of 1896, Lampman complains in his letter to Maud of 2 April 1896 that "Copeland & Day have issued Duncan's [Campbell Scott] book of stories 'In the Village of Viger', But I hear nothing of my book. They have treated me badly, but of course I have no redress, and cannot help myself." (Sommers, 109). And, again to Maud, 7 April 1896, he says "My book is not out yet and I am getting mad." (Sommers, 111).

Lyrics of Earth was released on 7 May 1896, and Lampman noted to Thomson on 25 June 1896 that "My little book does not appear to have excited any notice. I hear nothing of it. I think it is a good book nevertheless and will have its due later on." (Lynn, 173).

[20] Doubt and depression, occasioned by what he saw as a general indifference to his work, were added to the ills that plagued Lampman's precarious state of health. There is a steady refrain of resignation in his letters,perhaps best characterized by the two concluding sentences of his letter to Thomson of 20 July 1896. He says: "God knows what will be the result of me. I think I am less clear than ever on that point."

(Lynn, 175)

[21] 22 June 1897 was the Diamond Jubilee of Queen Victoria, and in observance of the event, the Royal Society of Canada sent her a telegram of congratulation.

[22] Lighthall Papers, Department of Rare Books and Special Collections, McGill University Libraries.

[23] Lighthall Papers, Department of Rare Books and Special Collections, McGill University Libraries.

[24] The electrification of cities, the expansion of railway travel and traffic, the motorcar, advances in photography, the cinema and the phonograph were some of the major technological and scientific developments of Lampman's time.

[25] See T.H. Huxley's (1825-1895) justly famous and influential lecture, *Evolution and Ethics* (1894) and H.G. Wells' (1866-1946) essay, "Human Evolution, and Artificial Process" October 1, 1896, *The Fortnightly Review.*

What may be relevant for an understanding of "The City of the End of Things" is that it was generally believed by physicists that the earth was gradually cooling, and that all forms of life would die out except for certain low species capable of survival in arctic or antarctic conditions. Could this be Lampman's surviving "idiot" facing the "lightless north" ?

THE POEMS

APRIL

Pale season, watcher in unvexed suspense,
Still priestess of the patient middle day,
Betwixt wild March's humored petulence
And the warm wooing of green kirtled May,
Maid month of sunny peace and sober grey,
Weaver of flowers in sunward glades that ring
With murmur of libation to the spring:

As memory of pain, all past, is peace,
And joy, dream-tasted, hath the deepest cheer,
So art thou sweetest of all months that lease
The twelve short spaces of the flying year.
The bloomless days are dead, and frozen fear
No more for many moons shall vex the earth,
Dreaming of summer and fruit laden mirth.

The grey song-sparrows full of spring have sung
Their clear thin silvery tunes in leafless trees;
The robin hops, and whistles, and among
The silver-tasseled poplars the brown bees
Murmur faint dreams of summer harvestries;
The creamy sun at even scatters down
A gold-green mist across the murmuring town.

By the slow streams the frogs all day and night
Dream without thought of pain or heed of ill,
Watching the long warm silent hours take flight,
And ever with soft throats that pulse and thrill,
From the pale-weeded shallows trill and trill,
Tremulous sweet voices, flute-like, answering
One to another glorying in the spring

All day across the ever-cloven soil,
Strong horses labour, steaming in the sun,
Down the long furrows with slow straining toil,
Turning the brown clean layers; and one by one
The crows gloom over them till daylight done
Finds them asleep somewhere in duskèd lines
Beyond the wheatlands in the northern pines.

The old year's cloaking of brown leaves, that bind
The forest floor-ways, plated close and true —
The last love's labour of the autumn wind —
Is broken with curled flower buds white and blue
In all the matted hollows, and speared through
With thousand serpent-spotted blades up-sprung,
Yet bloomless, of the slender adder-tongue.

In the warm noon the south wind creeps and cools,
Where the red-budded stems of maples throw
Still tangled etchings on the amber pools,
Quite silent now, forgetful of the slow
Drip of the taps, the troughs, and trampled snow,
The keen March mornings, and the silvering rime
And mirthful labour of the sugar prime.

Ah, I have wandered with unwearied feet,
All the long sweetness of an April day,
Lulled with cool murmurs and the drowsy beat
Of partridge wings in secret thickets grey,
The marriage hymns of all the birds at play,
The faces of sweet flowers, and easeful dreams
Beside slow reaches of frog-haunted streams;

Wandered with happy feet, and quite forgot
The shallow toil, the strife against the grain,
Near souls, that hear us call, but answer not,
The loneliness, perplexity and pain,
And high thoughts cankered with an earthly stain
And then the long draught emptied to the lees,
I turn me homeward in slow pacing ease,

Cleaving the cedar shadows and the thin
Mist of grey gnats that cloud the river shore,
Sweet even choruses, that dance and spin
Soft tangles in the sunset; and once more
The city smites me with its dissonant roar.
To its hot heart I pass, untroubled yet,
Fed with calm hope, without desire or fret.

So to the year's first altar step I bring
Gifts of meek song, and make my spirit free
With the blind working of unanxious spring,
Careless with her, whether the days that flee
Pale drouth or golden-fruited plenty see,
So that we toil, brothers, without distress,
In calm-eyed peace and godlike blamelessness.

THE FROGS

I

Breathers of wisdom won without a quest,
Quaint uncouth dreamers, voices high and strange,
Flutists of lands where beauty hath no change,
And wintery grief is a forgotten guest,
Sweet murmurers of everlasting rest,
For whom glad days have ever yet to run,
And moments are as aeons, and the sun
But ever sunken half-way toward the west.

Often to me who heard you in your day,
With close wrapt* ears, it could not choose but seem
That earth, our mother, searching in what way,
Men's hearts might know her spirit's inmost dream,
Ever at rest beneath life's change and stir,
Made you her soul, and bade you pipe for her.

II

In those mute days when spring was in her glee,
And hope was strong, we knew not why or how,
And earth, the mother, dreamed with brooding brow,
Musing on life, and what the hours might be,
When love should ripen to maternity,
Then like high flutes in silvery interchange
Ye piped with voices still and sweet and strange,
And ever as ye piped, on every tree

The great buds swelled; among the pensive woods
The spirits of first flowers awoke and flung
From buried faces the close fitting hoods,
And listened to your piping till they fell,
The frail spring-beauty with her perfumed bell,
The wind-flower, and the spotted adder-tongue.

III

All the day long, wherever pools might be
Among the golden meadows, where the air
Stood in a dream, as it were moorèd there
Forever in a noon-tide reverie,
Or where the birds made riot of their glee
In the still woods, and the hot sun shone down,
Crossed with warm lucent shadows on the brown
Leaf-paven pools, that bubbled dreamily,

Or far away in whispering river meads
And watery marshes where the brooding noon,
Full with the wonder of its own sweet boon,
Nestled and slept among the noiseless reeds,
Ye sat and murmured, motionless as they,
With eyes that dreamed beyond the night and day.

IV

And when day passed and over heaven's height,
Thin with the many stars and cool with dew,
The fingers of the deep hours slowly drew
The wonder of the ever-healing night,
No grief or loneliness or wrapt* delight
Or weight of silence ever brought to you
Slumber or rest; only your voices grew
More high and solemn; slowly with hushed flight

Ye saw the echoing hours go by, long-drawn,
Nor ever stirred, watching with fathomless eyes,
And with your countless clear antiphonies
Filling the earth and heaven, even till dawn,
Last-risen, found you with its first pale gleam,
Still with soft throats unaltered in your dream.

V

And slowly as we heard you, day by day,
The stillness of enchanted reveries
Bound brain and spirit and half-closed eyes,
In some divine sweet wonder-dream astray;
To us no sorrow or upreared dismay
Nor any discord came, but evermore
The voices of mankind, the outer roar,
Grew strange and murmurous, faint and far away.

Morning and noon and midnight exquisitely,
Wrapt with your voices, this alone we knew,
Cities might change and fall, and men might die,
Secure were we, content to dream with you,
That change and pain are shadows faint and fleet,
And dreams are real, and life is only sweet.

HEAT

From plains that reel to southward, dim,
    The road runs by me white and bare;
Up the steep hill it seems to swim
    Beyond, and melt into the glare.
Upward half way, or it may be
    Nearer the summit, slowly steals
A hay-cart, moving dustily
    With idly clacking wheels.

By his cart's side the wagoner
    Is slouching slowly at his ease,
Half-hidden in the windless blur
    Of white dust puffing to his knees.
This wagon on the height above,
    From sky to sky on either hand,
Is the sole thing that seems to move
    In all the heat-held land.

Beyond me in the fields the sun
    Soaks in the grass and hath his will;
I count the marguerites one by one;
    Even the buttercups are still.
On the brook yonder not a breath
    Disturbs the spider or the midge.
The water-bugs draw close beneath
    The cool gloom of the bridge.

Where the far elm-tree shadows flood
Dark patches in the burning grass,
The cows, each with her peaceful cud,
Lie waiting for the heat to pass.
From somewhere on the slope near by
Into the pale depth of the noon
A wandering thrush slides leisurely
His thin revolving tune.

In intervals of dreams I hear
The cricket from the droughty ground;
The grass-hoppers spin into mine ear
A small innumerable sound.
I lift mine eyes sometimes to gaze:
The burning sky-line blinds my sight:
The woods far off are blue with haze:
The hills are drenched in light.

And yet to me not this or that
Is always sharp or always sweet;
In the sloped shadow of my hat
I lean at rest, and drain the heat;
Nay more, I think some blessèd power
Hath brought me wandering idly here:
In the full furnace of this hour
My thoughts grow keen and clear.

AMONG THE TIMOTHY

Long hours ago, while yet the morn was blithe,
    Nor sharp athirst had drunk the beaded dew,
A reaper* came, and swung his cradled* scythe
    Around this stump, and, shearing slowly, drew
    Far round among the clover, ripe for hay,
        A circle clean and grey;
And here among the scented swathes that gleam,
    Mixed with dead daisies, it is sweet to lie
    And watch the grass and the few-clouded sky,
        Nor think but only dream.

For when the noon was turning, and the heat
    Fell down most heavily on field and wood,
I too came hither, borne on restless feet,
    Seeking some comfort for an aching mood.
    Ah, I was weary of the drifting hours,
        The echoing city towers,
The blind grey streets, the jingle of the throng,
    Weary of hope that like a shape of stone
    Sat near at hand without a smile or moan,
        And weary most of song.

And those high moods of mine that sometime made
    My heart a heaven, opening like a flower,
A sweeter world where I in wonder strayed,
    Begirt with shapes of beauty and the power
    Of dreams that moved through that enchanted clime
        With changing breaths of rhyme,
Were all gone lifeless now like those white leaves

That hang all winter, shivering dead and blind
Among the sinewy beeches in the wind,
That vainly calls and grieves.

Ah! I will set no more mine overtaskèd brain
To barren search and toil that beareth nought,
Forever following with sorefooted pain
The crossing pathways of unbournèd* thought;
But let it go, as one that hath no skill,
To take what shape it will,
An ant slow-burrowing in the earthy gloom,
A spider bathing in the dew at morn,
Or a brown bee in wayward fancy borne
From hidden bloom to bloom.

Hither and thither o'er the rocking grass
The little breezes, blithe as they are blind,
Teasing the slender blossoms pass and pass,
Soft-footed children of the gipsy wind,
To taste of every purple-fringèd head
Before the bloom is dead;
And scarcely heed the daisies that, endowed
With stems so short they cannot see, up-bear
Their innocent sweet eyes distressed, and stare
Like children in a crowd.

Not far to fieldward in the central heat,
Shadowing the clover, a pale poplar stands
With glimmering leaves that, whenthe wind comes, beat
Together like innumerable small hands,
And with the calm, as in vague dreams astray,
Hang wan and silver-grey;
Like sleepy maenads, who in pale surprise,
Half-wakenend by a prowling beast, have crept
Out of the hidden covert, where they slept,
At noon with languid eyes.

The crickets creak, and through the noonday glow,
That crazy fiddler of the hot mid-year,
The dry cicada plies his wiry bow
In long-spun cadence, thin and dusty sere:
From the green grass the small grasshoppers' din
Spreads soft and silvery thin:
And ever and anon a murmur steals
Into mine ears of toil that moves alway,
The crackling rustle of the pitch-forked hay
And lazy jerk of wheels.

As so I lie and feel the soft hours wane,
To wind and sun and peaceful sound laid bare,
That aching dim discomfort of the brain
Fades off unseen, and shadowy-footed care
Into some hidden corner creeps at last
To slumber deep and fast;
And gliding on, quite fashioned to forget,
From dream to dream I bid my spirit pass
Out into the pale green ever-swaying grass
To brood, but no more fret.

And hour by hour among all shapes that grow
Of purple mints and daisies gemmed with gold
In sweet unrest my visions come and go;
I feel and hear and with quiet eyes behold;
And hour by hour, the ever-journeying sun,
In gold and shadow spun,
Into mine eyes and blood, and through the dim
Green glimmering forest of the grass shines down,
Till flower and blade, and every cranny brown,
And I are soaked with him.

FREEDOM

Out of the heart of the city begotten
  Of the labour of men and their manifold hands,
Whose souls, that were sprung from the earth in her morning,
No longer regard or remember her warning,
  Whose hearts in the furnace of care have forgotten
    Forever the scent and the hue of her lands;

Out of the heat of the usurer's hold,
  From the horrible crash of the strong man's feet;
Out of the shadow where pity is dying;
Out of the clamour where beauty is lying,
  Dead in the depth of the struggle for gold;
  Out of the din and the glare of the street;

Into the arms of our mother we come,
  Our broad strong mother, the innocent earth,
Mother of all things beautiful, blameless,
Mother of hopes that her strength makes tameless,
  Where the voices of grief and of battle are dumb,
    And the whole world laughs with the light of her mirth.

Over the fields, where the cool winds sweep,
  Black with the mould and brown with the loam,
Where the thin green spears of the wheat are appearing,
And the high-ho shouts from the smoky clearing;
  Over the widths where the cloud shadows creep;
    Over the fields and the fallows we come;

Over the swamps with their pensive noises,
  Where the burnished cup of the marigold gleams;
Skirting the reeds, where the quick winds shiver
On the swelling breast of the dimpled river,
  And the blue of the king-fisher hangs and poises,
    Watching a spot by the edge of the streams;

By the miles of the fences warped and dyed
With the white-hot noons and their withering fires,
Where the rough bees trample the creamy bosoms
Of the hanging tufts of the elder blossoms,
And the spiders weave, and the grey snakes hide,
In the crannied gloom of the stones and the briers;

Over the meadow lands sprouting with thistle,
Where the humming wings of the blackbirds pass,
Where the hollows are banked with the violets flowering,
And the long-limbed pendulous elms are towering,
Where the robins are loud with their voluble whistle,
And the ground sparrow scurries away through the grass,

Where the restless bobolink loiters and woos
Down in the hollows and over the swells,
Dropping in and out of the shadows,
Sprinkling his music about the meadows,
Whistles and little checks and coos,
And the tinkle of glassy bells;

Into the dim woods full of the tombs
Of the dead trees soft in their sepulchres,
Where the pensive throats of the shy birds hidden,
Pipe to us strangely entering unbidden,
And tenderly still in the tremulous glooms
The trilliums scatter their white-winged stars;

Up to the hills where our tired hearts rest,
Loosen, and halt, and regather their dreams;
Up to the hills, where the winds restore us,
Clearing our eyes to the beauty before us,
Earth with the glory of life on her breast,
Earth with the gleam of her cities and streams.

Here we shall commune with her and no other;
Care and the battle of life shall cease;
Men her degenerate children behind us,
Only the might of her beauty shall bind us,
Full of rest, as we gaze on the face of our mother,
Earth in the health and the strength of her peace.

MORNING ON THE LIEVRES*

Far above us where a jay
Screams his matins to the day,
Capped with gold and amethyst,
Like a vapour from the forge
Of a giant somewhere hid,
Out of hearing of the clang
Of his hammer, skirts of mist
Slowly up the woody gorge
Lift and hang.

Softly as a cloud we go,
Sky above and sky below,
Down the river, and the dip
Of the paddles scarcely breaks,
With the little silvery drip
Of the water as it shakes
From the blades, the crystal deep
Of the silence of the morn,
Of the forest yet asleep,
And the river reaches borne
In a mirror, purple grey,
Sheer away
To the misty line of light,
Where the forest and the stream
In the shadow meet and plight,
Like a dream.

From amid a stretch of reeds,
Where the lazy river sucks
All the water as it bleeds
From a little curling creek,
And the muskrats peer and sneak
In around the sunken wrecks
Of a tree that swept the skies
Long ago,

On a sudden seven ducks
With a splashy rustle rise,
Stretching out their seven necks,
One before, and two behind,
And the others all arow,
And as steady as the wind
With a swivelling whistle go,
Through the purple shadow led,
Till we only hear their whir
In behind a rocky spur,
Just ahead.

IN OCTOBER

Along the waste, a great way off, the pines,
Like tall slim priests of storm, stand up and bar
The low long strip of dolorous red that lines
The under west, where wet winds moan afar.
The cornfields all are brown, and brown the meadows
With the blown leaves' wind-heapèd traceries,
And the brown thistle stems that cast no shadows,
And bear no bloom for bees.

As slowly earthward leaf by red leaf slips,
The sad trees rustle in chill misery,
A soft strange inner sound of pain-crazed lips,
That move and murmur incoherently;
As if all leaves, that yet have breath, were sighing,
With pale hushed throats, for death is at the door,
So many low soft masses for the dying
Sweet leaves that live no more.

Here I will sit upon this naked stone,
Draw my coat closer with my numbèd hands,
And hear the ferns sigh, and the wet woods moan,
And send my heart out to the ashen lands;
And I will ask myself what golden madness,
What balmèd breaths of dreamland spicery,
What visions of soft laughter and light sadness
Were sweet last month to me.

The dry dead leaves flit by with thin weird tunes,
Like failing murmurs of some conquered creed,
Graven in mystic markings with strange runes,*
That none but stars and biting winds may read;
Here I will wait a little; I am weary,
Not torn with pain of any lurid hue,
But only still and very grey and dreary,
Sweet sombre lands, like you.

WINTER

The long days came and went; the riotous bees
Tore the warm grapes in many a dusty vine,
And men grew faint and thin with too much ease,
And Winter gave no sign:
But all the while beyond the northmost woods
He sat and smiled and watched his spirits play
In elfish dance and eery roundelay,
Tripping in many moods
With snowy curve and fairy crystal shine.

But now the time is come: with southward speed
The elfin spirits pass: a secret sting
Hath fallen and smitten flower and fruit and weed,
And every leafy thing.
The wet woods moan: the dead leaves break and fall;
In still night- watches wakeful men have heard
The muffled pipe of many a passing bird,
High over hut and hall,
Straining to southward with unresting wing.

And then they come with colder feet, and fret
The winds with snow, and tuck the streams to sleep
With icy sheet and gleaming coverlet,
And fill the valleys deep
With curvèd drifts, and a strange music raves
Among the pines, sometimes in wails, and then
In whistled laughter, till affrighted men
Draw close, and into caves
And earthy holes the blind beasts curl and creep.

And so all day above the toiling heads
Of men's poor chimneys, full of impish freaks,
Tearing and twisting in tight-curlèd shreds
The vain unnumbered reeks,
The Winter speeds his fairies forth and mocks
Poor bitten men with laughter icy cold,
Turning the brown of youth to white and old
With hoary-woven locks,
And grey men young with roses in their cheeks.

And after thaws, when liberal water swells
The bursting eaves, he biddeth drip and grow
The curly horns of ribbèd icicles
In many a beard-like row.
In secret moods of mercy and soft dole,
Old warpèd wrecks and things of mouldering death
That summer scorns and man abandoneth
His careful hands console
With lawny robes and draperies of snow.

And when night comes, his spirits with chill feet,
Winged with white mirth and noiseless mockery,
Across men's pallid windows peer and fleet,
And smiling silverly
Draw with mute fingers on the frosted glass
Quaint fairy shapes of icèd witcheries,
Pale flowers and glinting ferns and frigid trees
And meads of mystic grass,
Graven in many an austere phantasy.

But far away the Winter dreams alone,
Rustling among his snow-drifts, and resigns
Cold fondling ears to hear the cedars moan
In dusky-skirted lines
Strange answers of an ancient runic call;
Or somewhere watches with his antique eyes,
Grey-chill with frosty-lidded reveries,
The silvery moonshine fall
In misty wedges through his girth of pines.

Poor mortals haste and hide away: creep soon
Into your icy beds: the embers die;
And on your frosted panes the pallid moon
Is glimmering brokenly.
Mutter faint prayers that spring will come e'erwhile,
Scarring with thaws and dripping days and nights
The shining majesty of him that smites
And slays you with a smile
Upon his silvery lips, of glinting mockery.

WINTER HUES RECALLED

Life is not all for effort: there are hours,
When fancy breaks from the exacting will,
And rebel thought takes schoolboy's holiday,
Rejoicing in its idle strength. 'Tis then,
And only at such moments, that we know
The treasure of hours gone — scenes once beheld,
Sweet voices and words bright and beautiful,
Impetuous deeds that woke the God within us,
The loveliness of forms and thoughts and colors,
A moment marked and then as soon forgotten.
These things are ever near us, laid away,
Hidden and waiting the appropriate times,
In the quiet garner-house of memory.
There in the silent unaccounted depth,
Beneath the heated strainage and the rush
That teem the noisy surface of the hours,
All things that ever touched us are stored up,
Growing more mellow like sealed wine with age;
We thought them dead, and they are but asleep.
In moments when the heart is most at rest
And least expectant, from the luminous doors,
And sacred dwelling place of things unfeared,
They issue forth, and we who never knew
Till then how potent and how real they were,
Take them, and wonder, and so bless the hour.

Such gifts are sweetest when unsought. To me,
As I was loitering lately in my dreams,
Passing from one remembrance to another,
Like him who reads upon an outstretched map,
Content and idly happy, these rose up,
Out of that magic well-stored picture house,
No dream, rather a thing most keenly real,

The memory of a moment, when with feet,
Arrested and spell bound, and captured eyes,
Made wide with joy and wonder, I beheld
The spaces of a white and wintery land
Swept with the fire of sunset, all its width
Vale, forest, town, and misty eminence,
A miracle of color and of beauty.

I had walked out, as I remember now,
With covered ears, for the bright air was keen,
To southward up the gleaming snow-packed fields,
With the snowshoer's long rejoicing stride,
Marching at ease. It was a radiant day
In February, the month of the great struggle
'Twixt sun and frost, when with advancing spears,
The glittering golden vanguard of the spring
Holds the broad winter's yet unbroken rear
In long-closed wavering contest. Thin pale threads
Like streaks of ash across the far off blue
Were drawn, nor seemed to move. A brooding silence
Kept all the land, a stillness as of sleep;
But in the east the grey and motionless woods,
Watching the great sun's fiery slow decline,
Grew deep with gold. To westward all was silver.
An hour had passed above me; I had reached
The loftiest level of the snow-piled fields,
Clear-eyed, but unobservant, noting not,
That all the plain beneath me and the hills
Took on a change of color splendid, gradual,
Leaving no spot the same; nor that the sun
Now like a fiery torrent overflamed
The great line of the west. Ere yet I turned
With long stride homeward, being heated
With the loose swinging motion, weary too,
Nor uninclined to rest, a buried fence,
Whose topmost log just shouldered from the snow,
Made me a seat, and thence with heated cheeks,
Grazed by the northwind's edge of stinging ice,
I looked far out upon the snow-bound waste,

The lifting hills and intersecting forests,
The scarce marked courses of the buried streams,
And as I looked lost memory of the frost,
Transfixed with wonder, overborne with joy.
I saw them in their silence and their beauty,
Swept by the sunset's rapid hand of fire,
Sudden, mysterious, every moment deepening
To some new majesty of rose or flame.
The whole broad west was like a molten sea
Of crimson. In the north the light-lined hills
Were veiled far off as with a mist of rose
Wondrous and soft. Along the darkening east
The gold of all the forests slowly changed
To purple. In the valley far before me,
Low sunk in sapphire shadows, from its hills,
Softer and lovelier than an opening flower,
Uprose a city with its sun-touched towers,
A bunch of amethysts.

Like one spell-bound
Caught in the presence of some god, I stood,
Nor felt the keen wind and the deadly air,
But watched the sun go down, and watched the gold
Fade from the town and the withdrawing hills,
Their westward shapes athwart the dusky red
Freeze into sapphire, saw the arc of rose
Rise ever higher in the violet east,
Above the frore front of the uprearing night
Remorsefully soft and sweet. Then I awoke
As from a dream, and from my shoulders shook
The warning chill, till then unfelt, unfeared.

DESPONDENCY

Slow figures in some live remorseless frieze,
　　The approaching days escapeless and unguessed,
　　With mask and shroud impenetrably dressed;
Time, whose inexorable destinies
Bear down upon us like impending seas;
　　And the huge presence of this world, at best
　　A sightless giant wandering without rest,
Agèd and mad with many miseries.

The weight and measure of these things who knows ?
　　Resting at times beside life's thought-swept stream,
Sobered and stunned with unexpected blows,
　　We scarcely hear the uproar; life doth seem,
Save for the certain nearness of its woes,
　　Vain and phantasmal as a sick man's dream.

GENTLENESS

Blind multitudes that jar confusedly
        At strife, earth's children, will ye never rest
        From toils made hateful here, and dawns distressed
With ravelling self-engendered misery?
And will ye never know, till sleep shall see
        Your graves, how dreadful and how dark indeed
        Are pride, self-will, and blind-voiced anger, greed,
And malice with its subtle cruelty?

How beautiful is gentleness, whose face
        Like April sunshine, or the summer rain,
    Swells everywhere the buds of generous thought?
So easy, and so sweet it is; its grace
        Smoothes out so soon the tangled knots of pain.
    Can ye not learn it? will ye not be taught?

THE TRUTH

Friend, though thy soul should burn thee, yet be still.
  Thoughts were not meant for strife, nor tongues for swords
  He that sees clear is gentlest of his words,
And that's not truth that hath the heart to kill.
The whole world's thought shall not one truth fulfil.
  Dull in our age, and passionate in youth,
  No mind of man hath found the perfect truth,
Nor shalt thou find it; therefore, friend be still.

Watch and be still, nor hearken to the fool,
The babbler of consistency and rule:
  Wisest is he, who, never quite secure,
    Changes his thoughts for better day by day:
  To-morrow some new light will shine, be sure,
    And thou shalt see thy thought another way.

A NIGHT OF STORM

Oh city, whom grey stormy hands have sown
    With restless drift, scarce broken now of any,
    Out of the dark thy windows dim and many
Gleam red across the storm. Sound is there none,
Save evermore the fierce wind's sweep and moan,
    From whose grey hands the keen white snow is shaken
    In desperate gusts, that fitfully lull and waken,
Dense as night's darkness round thy towers of stone.

Darkling and strange art thou thus vexed and chidden;*
    More dark and strange thy veilèd agony,
City of storm, in whose grey heart are hidden
    What stormier woes, what lives that groan and beat,
    Stern and thin-cheeked, against time's heavier sleet,
      Rude fates, hard hearts, and prisoning poverty.

THE RAILWAY STATION

The darkness brings no quiet here, the light
No waking: ever on my blinded brain
The flare of lights, the rush , and cry, and strain,
The engines' scream, the hiss and thunder smite:
I see the hurrying crowds, the clasp, the flight,
Faces that touch, eyes that are dim with pain:
I see the hoarse wheels turn, and the great train
Move labouring out into the bourneless* night.

So many souls within its dim recesses,
So many bright, so many mournful eyes:
Mine eyes that watch grow fixed with dreams and guesses;
What threads of life, what hidden histories,
What sweet or passionate dreams and dark distresses,
What unknown thoughts, what various agonies!

IN NOVEMBER

The hills and leafless forests slowly yield
To the thick-driving snow. A little while
And night shall darken down. In shouting file
The woodmen's carts go by me homeward-wheeled,
Past the thin fading stubbles, half-concealed,
Now golden-grey, sowed softly through with snow,
Where the last ploughman follows still his row,
Turning black furrows through the whitening field.

Far off the village lamps begin to gleam,
Fast drives the snow, and no man comes this way;
The hills grow wintery white, and bleak winds moan
About the naked uplands. I alone
Am neither sad, nor shelterless, nor grey,
Wrapped round with thought, content to watch and dream.

THE CITY

Beyond the dusky corn-fields, toward the west,
    Dotted with farms, beyond the shallow stream,
    Through drifts of elm with quite peep and gleam,
Curved white and slender as a lady's wrist,
Faint and far off out of the autumn mist,
    Even as a pointed jewel softly set
    In clouds of colour warmer, deeper yet,
Crimson and gold and rose and amethyst,
Toward dayset, where the journeying sun grown old
Hangs lowly westward darker now than gold,
With the soft sun-touch of the yellowing hours
    Made lovelier, I see with dreaming eyes,
    Even as a dream out of a dream, arise
The bell-tongued city with its glorious towers.

SOLITUDE

How still it is here in the woods. The trees
Stand motionless, as if they did not dare
To stir, lest it should break the spell. The air
Hangs quiet as spaces in a marble frieze.*
Even this little brook, that runs at ease,
Whispering and gurgling in its knotted bed,
Seems but to deepen with its curling thread
Of sound the shadowy sun-pierced silences.

Sometimes a hawk screams or a woodpecker
Startles the stillness from its fixèd mood
With his loud careless tap. Sometimes I hear
The dreamy white-throat from some far off tree
Pipe slowly on the listening solitude
His five pure notes succeeding pensively.

APRIL IN THE HILLS

To-day the world is wide and fair
With sunny fields of lucid air,
And waters dancing everywhere;
The snow is almost gone;
The noon is builded high with light,
And over heaven's liquid height,
In steady fleets serene and white,
The happy clouds go on.

The channels run, the bare earth steams,
And every hollow rings and gleams
With jetting falls and dashing streams;
The rivers burst and fill;
The fields are full of little lakes,
And when the romping wind awakes
The water ruffles blue and shakes,
And the pines roar on the hill.

The crows go by, a noisy throng;
About the meadows all day long
The shore-lark drops his brittle song;
And up the leafless tree
The nut-hatch runs, and nods, and clings;
The bluebird dips with flashing wings,
The robin flutes, the sparrow sings,
And the swallows float and flee.

I break the spirit's cloudy bands,
A wanderer in enchanted lands,
I feel the sun upon my hands;
And far from care and strife
The broad earth bids me forth. I rise

With lifted brow and upward eyes.
I bathe my spirit in blue skies,
        And taste the springs of life.

I feel the tumult of new birth;
I waken with the wakening earth;
I match the bluebird in her mirth;
        And wild with wind and sun,
A treasurer of immortal days,
I roam the glorious world with praise,
The hillsides and the woodland ways,
        Till earth and I are one.

LIFE AND NATURE

I passed through the gates of the city,
The streets were strange and still,
Through the doors of the open churches
The organs were moaning shrill.

Through the doors and the great high windows
I heard the murmur of prayer,
And the sound of their solemn singing
Streamed out on the sunlit air;

A sound of some great burden
That lay on the world's dark breast,
Of the old, and the sick, and the lonely,
And the weary that cried for rest.

I strayed through the midst of the city
Like one distracted or mad.
"Oh, Life! Oh, Life!" I kept saying,
And the very word seemed sad.

I passed through the gates of the city,
And I heard the small birds sing,
I laid me down in the meadows
Afar from the bell-ringing.

In the depth and the bloom of the meadows
I lay on the earth's quiet breast,
The poplar fanned me with shadows,
And the veery* sang me to rest.

Blue, blue was the heaven above me,
And the earth green at my feet;
"Oh, Life! Oh, Life!" I kept saying,
And the very word seemed sweet.

AFTER RAIN

For three whole days across the sky,
In sullen packs that loomed and broke,
With flying fringes dim as smoke,
The columns of the rain went by;
At every hour the wind awoke;
        The darkness passed upon the plain;
        The great drops rattled at the pane.

Now piped the wind, or far aloof
Fell to a sough remote and dull;
And all night long with rush and lull
The rain kept drumming on the roof:
I heard till ear and sense were full
        The clash or silence of the leaves,
        The gurgle in the creaking eaves.

But when the fourth day came — at noon,
The darkness and the rain were by;
The sunward roofs were steaming dry;
And all the world was flecked and strewn
With shadows from a fleecy sky.
        The haymakers were forth and gone,
        And every rillet laughed and shone.

Then , too, on me that loved so well
The world, despairing in her blight,
Uplifted with her least delight,
On me, as on the earth, there fell
New happiness of mirth and might;
        I strode the valleys pied and still;
        I climbed upon the breezy hill.

I watched the grey hawk wheel and drop,
Sole shadow on the shining world;
I saw the mountains clothed and curled,
With forest ruffling to the top;
I saw the river's length unfurled,
    Pale silver down the fruited plain,
    Grown great and stately with the rain.

Through miles of shadow and soft heat,
Where field and fallow, fence and tree,
Were all one world of greenery,
I heard the robin ringing sweet,
The sparrow piping silverly,
    The thrushes at the forest's hem;
    And as I went I sang with them.

COMFORT OF THE FIELDS

What would'st thou have for easement after grief,
    When the rude world hath used thee with despite,
    And care sits at thine elbow day and night,
Filching thy pleasures like a subtle thief?
To me, when life besets me in such wise,
'Tis sweetest to break forth, to drop the chain,
    And grasp the freedom of this pleasant earth,
    To roam in idleness and sober mirth,
Through summer airs and summer lands, and drain
The comfort of wide fields unto tired eyes.

By hills and waters, farms and solitudes,
    To wander by the day with wilful feet;
    Through fielded valleys wide with yellowing wheat;
Along grey roads that run between deep woods,
Murmurous and cool; through hallowed slopes of pine,
    Where the long daylight dreams, unpierced, unstirred,
    And only the rich-throated thrush is heard;
By lonely forest brooks that froth and shine
    In bouldered crannies buried in the hills;
By broken beeches tangled with wild vine,
    And log-strewn rivers murmurous with mills.

In upland pastures, sown with gold, and sweet
    With the keen perfume of the ripening grass,
    Where wings of birds and filmy shadows pass,
Spread thick as stars with shining marguerite;
To haunt old fences overgrown with brier,
    Muffled in vines, and hawthorns, and wild cherries,
    Rank poisonous ivies, red-bunched elderberries,
And pièd* blossoms to the heart's desire,
    Grey mullein towering into yellow bloom,

Pink-tasseled milkweed, breathing dense perfume,
And swarthy vervain, tipped with violet fire.

To hear at eve the bleating of far flocks,
The mud-hen's whistle from the marsh at morn;
To skirt with deafened ears and brain o'erborne
Some foam-filled rapid charging down its rocks
With iron roar of waters; far away
Across wide-reeded meres,* pensive with noon,
To hear the querulous outcry of the loon;
To lie among deep rocks, and watch all day
On liquid heights the snowy clouds melt by;
Or hear from wood-capped mountain-brows the jay
Pierce the bright morning with his jibing cry.

To feast on summer sounds; the jolted wains,*
The thrasher* humming from the farm near by,
The prattling cricket's intermittent cry,
The locust's rattle from the sultry lanes;
Or in the shadow of some oaken spray,
To watch, as through a mist of light and dreams,
The far-off hay-fields, where the dusty teams
Drive round and round the lessening squares of hay,
And hear upon the wind, now loud, now low,
With drowsy cadence half a summer's day,
The clatter of the reapers come and go.

Far violet hills, horizons filmed with showers,
The murmur of cool streams, the forest's gloom,
The voices of the breathing grass, the hum
Of ancient gardens overbanked with flowers:
Thus, with a smile as golden as the dawn,
And cool fair fingers radiantly divine,
The mighty mother brings us in her hand,
For all tired eyes and foreheads pinched and wan,
Her restful cup, her beaker of bright wine:
Drink, and be filled, and ye shall understand!

SEPTEMBER

Now hath the summer reached her golden close,
And, lost amid her corn-fields, bright of soul,
Scarcely perceives from her divine repose
How near, how swift, the inevitable goal:
Still, still, she smiles, though from her careless feet
The bounty and the fruitful strength are gone,
And through the soft long wondering days goes on
The silent sere decadence sad and sweet.

The kingbird and the pensive thrush are fled,
Children of light, too fearful of the gloom;
The sun falls low, the secret word is said,
The mouldering woods grow silent as the tomb;
Even the fields have lost their sovereign grace,
The cone-flower and the marguerite; and no more,
Across the river's shadow-haunted floor,
The paths of skimming swallows interlace.

Already in the outland wilderness
The forests echo with unwonted dins;
In clamorous gangs the gathering woodmen press
Northward, and the stern winter's toil begins.
Around the long low shanties, whose rough lines
Break the sealed dreams of many an unnamed lake,
Already in the frost-clear morns awake
The crash and thunder of the falling pines.

Where the tilled earth, with all its fields set free,
Naked and yellow from the harvest lies,
By many a loft and busy granary,
The hum and tumult of the thrashers rise;
There the tanned farmers labour without slack,
Till twilight deepens round the spouting mill,
Feeding the loosened sheaves, or with fierce will,
Pitching waist-deep upon the dusty stack.

Still a brief while, ere the old year quite pass,
    Our wandering steps and wistful eyes shall greet
The leaf, the water, the beloved grass;
    Still from these haunts and this accustomed seat
I see the wood-wrapt city, swept with light,
    The blue long-shadowed distance, and, between,
    The dotted farm-lands with their parcelled green,
The dark pine forest and the watchful height.

I see the broad rough meadow stretched away
    Into the crystal sunshine, wastes of sod,
Acres of withered vervain, purple-grey,
    Branches of aster, groves of goldenrod;
And yonder, toward the sunlit summit, strewn
    With shadowy boulders, crowned and swathed with weed,
    Stand ranks of silken thistles, blown to seed,
Long silver fleeces shining like the noon.

In far-off russet corn-fields, where the dry
    Grey shocks stand peaked and withering, half concealed
In the rough earth, the orange pumpkins lie,
    Full-ribbed; and in the windless pasture-field
The sleek red horses o'er the sun-warmed ground
    Stand pensively about in companies,
    While all around them from the motionless trees
The long clean shadows sleep without a sound.

Under cool elm-trees floats the distant stream,
    Moveless as air; and o'er the vast warm earth
The fathomless daylight seems to stand and dream,
    A liquid cool elixir — all its girth
Bound with faint haze, a frail transparency,
    Whose lucid purple barely veils and fills
    The utmost valleys and the thin last hills,
Nor mars one whit their perfect clarity.

Thus without grief the golden days go by,
    So soft we scarcely notice how they wend,
And like a smile half happy, or a sigh,
    The summer passes to her quiet end;
And soon, too soon, around the cumbered eaves
    Sly frosts shall take the creepers by surprise,
    And through the wind-touched reddening woods shall rise
October with the rain of ruined leaves.

AN AUTUMN LANDSCAPE

No wind there is that either pipes or moans;
    The fields are cold and still; the sky
        Is covered with a blue-grey sheet
        Of motionless cloud; and at my feet
    The river, curling softly by,
Whispers and dimples round its quiet grey stones.

Along the chill green slope that dips and heaves
    The road runs rough and silent, lined
        With plum-trees, misty and blue-grey,
        And poplars pallid as the day,
    In masses spectral, undefined,
Pale greenish stems half hid in dry grey leaves.

And on beside the river's sober edge
    A long fresh field lies black. Beyond,
        Low thickets grey and reddish stand,
        Stroked white with birch; and near at hand,
    Over a little steel-smooth pond,
Hang multitudes of thin and withering sedge.

Across a waste and solitary rise
    A ploughman urges his dull team,
        A stooped grey figure with prone brow

That plunges bending to the plough
With strong, uneven steps. The stream
Rings and re-echoes with his furious cries.

Sometimes the lowing of a cow, long-drawn,
Comes from far off; and crows in strings
Pass on the upper silences.
A flock of small grey goldfinches,
Flown down with silvery twitterings,
Rustle among the birch-cones and are gone.

This day the season seems like one that heeds,
With fixèd ear and lifted hand,
All moods that yet are known on earth,
All motions that have faintest birth,
If haply she may understand
The utmost inward sense of all her deeds.

IN NOVEMBER

With loitering step and quiet eye,
Beneath the low November sky,
I wandered in the woods, and found
A clearing, where the broken ground
Was scattered with black stumps and briers,
And the old wreck of forest fires.
It was a bleak and sandy spot,
And, all about, the vacant plot
Was peopled and inhabited
By scores of mulleins long since dead.
A silent and forsaken brood
In that mute opening of the wood,
So shrivelled and so thin they were,
So grey, so haggard, and austere,
Not plants at all they seemed to me,
But rather some spare company
Of hermit folk, who long ago,
Wandering in bodies to and fro,
Had chanced upon this lonely way,
And rested thus, till death one day
Surprised them at their compline prayer,
And left them standing lifeless there.

There was no sound about the wood
Save the wind's secret stir. I stood
Among the mullein-stalks as still
As if myself had grown to be
One of their sombre company,
A body without wish or will.
And as I stood, quite suddenly,
Down from a furrow in the sky

The sun shone out a little space
Across that silent sober place,
Over the sand heaps and brown sod,
The mulleins and dead goldenrod,
And passed beyond the thickets grey,
And lit the fallen leaves that lay,
Level and deep within the wood,
A rustling yellow multitude.

And all around me the thin light,
So sere, so melancholy bright,
Fell like the half-reflected gleam
Or shadow of some former dream;
A moment's golden reverie
Poured out on every plant and tree
A semblance of weird joy, or less,
A sort of spectral happiness;
And I, too, standing idly there,
With muffled hands in the chill air,
Felt the warm glow about my feet,
And shuddering betwixt cold and heat,
Drew my thoughts closer, like a cloak,
While something in my blood awoke,
A nameless and unnatural cheer,
A pleasure secret and austere.

SNOWBIRDS

Along the narrow sandy height
I watch them swiftly come and go,
Or round the leafless wood,
Like flurries of wind-driven snow,
Revolving in perpetual flight,
A changing multitude.

Nearer and nearer still they sway,
And, scattering in a circled sweep,
Rush down without a sound;
And now I see them peer and peep,
Across yon level bleak and grey,
Searching the frozen ground, —

Until a little wind upheaves,
And makes a sudden rustling there,
And then they drop their play,
Flash up into the sunless air,
And like a flight of silver leaves
Swirl round and sweep away.

ALCYONE*

In the silent depth of space,
Immeasurably old, immeasurably far,
Glittering with a silver flame
Through eternity,
Rolls a great and burning star,
With a noble name,
            Alcyone!

In the glorious chart of heaven
It is marked the first of seven;
`Tis a Pleiad:*
And a hundred years of earth
With their long-forgotten deeds have come and gone,
Since that tiny point of light,
Once a splendour fierce and bright,
Had its birth
In the star we gaze upon.

It has travelled all that time —
Thought has not a swifter flight —
Through a region where no faintest gust
Of life comes ever, but the power of night
Dwells stupendous and sublime,
Limitless and void and lonely,
A region mute with age, and peopled only
With the dead and ruined dust
Of worlds that lived eternities ago.

Man! when thou dost think of this,
And what our earth and its existence is,
The half-blind toils since life began,
The little aims, the little span,
With what passion and what pride,
And what hunger fierce and wide,
Thou dost break beyond it all,
Seeking for the spirit unconfined
In the clear abyss of mind
A shelter and a peace majestical.
For what is life to thee,
Turning toward the primal light,
With that stern and silent face,
If thou canst not be
Something radiant and august as night,
Something wide as space?

Therefore with a love and gratitude divine
Thou shalt cherish in thine heart for sign
A vision of the great and burning star,
Immeasurably old, immeasurably far,
Surging forth its silver flame
Through eternity;
And thine inner heart shall ring and cry
With the music strange and high,
The grandeur of its name
Alycone!

THE CITY OF THE END OF THINGS

Beside the pounding cataracts
Of midnight streams unknown to us
'Tis builded in the leafless tracts
And valleys huge of Tartarus.*
Lurid and lofty and vast it seems;
It hath no rounded name that rings,
But I have heard it called in dreams
The City of the End of Things.

Its roofs and iron towers have grown
None knoweth how high within the night,
But in its murky streets far down
A flaming terrible and bright
Shakes all the stalking shadows there,
Across the walls, across the floors,
And shifts upon the upper air
From out a thousand furnace doors;
And all the while an awful sound
Keeps roaring on continually,
And crashes in the ceaseless round
Of a gigantic harmony.
Through its grim depths re-echoing
And all its weary height of walls,
With measured roar and iron ring,
The inhuman music lifts and falls.
Where no thing rests and no man is,
And only fire and night hold sway;
The beat, the thunder and the hiss
Cease not, and change not, night nor day.

And moving at unheard commands,
The abysses and vast fires between,
Flit figures that with clanking hands
Obey a hideous routine;
They are not flesh, they are not bone,
They see not with the human eye,
And from their iron lips is blown
A dreadful and monotonous cry;
And whoso of our mortal race
Should find that city unaware,
Lean Death would smite him face to face,
And blanch him with its venomed air:
Or caught by the terrific spell,
Each thread of memory snapt and cut,
His soul would shrivel and its shell
Go rattling like an empty nut.

It was not always so, but once,
In days that no man thinks upon,
Fair voices echoed from its stones,
The light above it leaped and shone:
Once there were multitudes of men,
That built that city in their pride,
Until its might was made, and then
They withered age by age and died.
But now of that prodigious race,
Three only in an iron tower,
Set like carved idols face to face,
Remain the masters of its power;
And at the city gate a fourth,
Gigantic and with dreadful eyes,
Sits looking toward the lightless north,
Beyond the reach of memories;
Fast rooted to the lurid floor,
A bulk that never moves a jot,
In his pale body dwells no more,
Or mind, or soul, — an idiot!

But sometime in the end those three
Shall perish and their hands be still,
And with the master's touch shall flee
Their incommunicable skill.
A stillness absolute as death
Along the slacking wheels shall lie,
And, flagging at a single breath,
The fires shall moulder out and die.
The roar shall vanish at its height,
And over that tremendous town
The silence of eternal night
Shall gather close and settle down.
All its grim grandeur, tower and hall,
Shall be abandoned utterly,
And into rust and dust shall fall
From century to century;
Nor ever living thing shall grow,
Or trunk of tree, or blade of grass;
No drop shall fall, no wind shall blow,
Nor sound of any foot shall pass:
Alone of its accursèd state,
One thing the hand of Time shall spare,
For the grim Idiot at the gate
Is deathless and eternal there.

PERSONALITY

O differing human heart,
Why is it that I tremble when thine eyes,
Thy human eyes and beautiful human speech,
Draw me, and stir within my soul
That subtle ineradicable longing
For tender comradeship?
It is because I cannot all at once,
Through the half-lights and phantom-haunted mists
That separate and enshroud us life from life,
Discern the nearness or the strangeness of thy paths
Nor plumb thy depths.
I am like one that comes alone at night
To a strange stream, and by an unknown ford
Stands, and for a moment yearns and shrinks,
Being ignorant of the water, though so quiet it is,
So softly murmurous,
So silvered by the familiar moon.

THE CLEARER SELF

Before me grew the human soul,
  And after I am dead and gone,
Through grades of effort and control
  The marvellous work shall still go on.

Each mortal in his little span
  Hath only lived, if he have shown
What greatness there can be in man
  Above the measured and the known;

How through the ancient layers of night,
  In gradual victory secure,
Grows ever with increasing light
  The Energy serene and pure:

The Soul, that from a monstrous past,
  From age to age, from hour to hour,
Feels upward to some height at last
  Of unimagined grace and power.

Though yet the sacred fire be dull,
  In folds of thwarting matter furled,
Ere death be nigh, while life is full,
  O Master Spirit of the world,

Grant me to know, to seek, to find,
  In some small measure though it be,
Emerging from the waste and blind,
  The clearer self, the grander me!

TO THE PROPHETIC SOUL

What are these bustlers at the gate
Of now or yesterday,
These playthings in the hand of Fate,
That pass, and point no way;

These clinging bubbles whose mock fires
For ever dance and gleam,
Vain foam that gathers and expires
Upon the world's dark stream;

These gropers betwixt right and wrong,
That seek an unknown goal,
Most ignorant, when they seem most strong;
What are they, then, O Soul,

That thou shouldst covet overmuch
A tenderer range of heart,
And yet at every dreamed-of touch
So tremulously start?

Thou with that hatred ever new
Of the world's base control,
That vision of the large and true,
That quickness of the soul;

Nay, for they are not of thy kind,
But in a rarer clay
God dowered thee with an alien mind;
Thou canst not be as they.

Be strong therefore; resume thy load,
And forward stone by stone
Go singing, though the glorious road
Thou travellest alone.

THE LAND OF PALLAS*

Methought I journeyed along ways that led for ever
Throughout a happy land where strife and care were dead,
And life went by me flowing like a placid river
Past sandy eyots where the shifting shoals make head.

A land where beauty dwelt supreme, and right, the donor
Of peaceful days; a land of equal gifts and deeds,
Of limitless fair fields and plenty had with honour;
A land of kindly tillage and untroubled meads,

Of gardens, and great fields, and dreaming rose-wreathed alleys,
Wherein at dawn and dusk the vesper sparrows sang;
Of cities set far off on hills down vista'd valleys,
And floods so vast and old, men wist* not whence they sprang,

Of groves, and forest depths, and fountains softly welling,
And roads that ran soft-shadowed past the open doors
Of mighty palaces and many a lofty dwelling,
Where all men entered and no master trod their floors.

A land of lovely speech, where every tone was fashioned
By generations of emotion high and sweet,
Of thought and deed and bearing lofty and impassioned;
A land of golden calm, grave forms, and fretless feet.

And every mode and saying of that land gave token
Of limits where no death or evil fortune fell,
And men lived out long lives in proud content unbroken,
For there no man was rich, none poor, but all were well.

And all the earth was common, and no base contriving
    Of money of coined gold was needed there or known,
But all men wrought together without greed or striving,
    And all the store of all to each man was his own.

From all that busy land, grey town, and peaceful village,
    Where never jar was heard, nor wail, nor cry of strife,
From every laden stream and all the fields of tillage,
    Arose the murmur and the kindly hum of life.

At morning to the fields came forth the men, each neighbour
    Hand linked to other, crowned, with wreaths upon their hair,
And all day long with joy they gave their hands to labour,
    Moving at will, unhastened, each man to his share.

At noon the women came, the tall fair women, bearing
    Baskets of wicker in their ample hands for each,
And learned the day's brief tale, and how the fields were faring,
    And blessed them with their lofty beauty and blithe speech.

And when the great day's toil was over, and the shadows
    Grew with the flocking stars, the sound of festival
Rose in each city square, and all the country meadows,
    Palace, and paven court, and every rustic hall.

Beside smooth streams, where alleys and green gardens meeting
    Ran downward to the flood with marble steps, a throng
Came forth of all the folk, at even, gaily greeting,
    With echo of sweet converse, jest, and stately song.

In all their great fair cities there was neither seeking
    For power of gold, nor greed of lust, nor desperate pain
Of multitudes that starve, or, in hoarse anger breaking,
    Beat at the doors of princes, break and fall in vain.

But all the children of that peaceful land, like brothers,
Lofty of spirit, wise, and ever set to learn
The chart of neighbouring souls, the bent and need of others,
Thought only of good deeds, sweet speech, and just return.

And there there was no prison, power of arms, nor palace,
Where prince or judge held sway, for none was needed there;
Long ages since the very names of fraud and malice
Had vanished from men's tongues, and died from all men's ca

And there there were no bonds of contract, deed, or marriage,
No oath, nor any form, to make the word more sure,
For no man dreamed of hurt, dishonour, or miscarriage,
Where every thought was truth, and every heart was pure.

There were no castes of rich or poor, of slave or master,
Where all were brothers, and the curse of gold was dead,
But all that wise fair race to kindlier ends and vaster
Moved on together with the same majestic tread.

And all the men and women of that land were fairer
Than even the mightiest of our meaner race can be;
The men like gentle children, great of limb, yet rarer
For wisdom and high thought, like kings for majesty.

And all the women through great ages of bright living,
Grown goodlier of stature, strong, and subtly wise,
Stood equal with the men, calm counsellors, ever giving
The fire and succour of proud faith and dauntless eyes.

And as I journeyed in that land I reached a ruin,
The gateway of a lonely and secluded waste,
A phantom of forgotten time and ancient doing,
Eaten by age and violence, crumbled and defaced.

On its grim outer walls the ancient world's sad glories
Were recorded in fire; upon its inner stone,
Drawn by dead hands, I saw, in tales and tragic stories,
The woe and sickness of an age of fear made known.

And lo, in that grey storehouse, fallen to dust and rotten,
Lay piled the traps and engines of forgotten greed,
The tomes of codes and canons, long disused, forgotten,
The robes and sacred books of many a vanished creed.

An old grave man I found, white-haired and gently spoken,
Who, as I questioned, answered with a smile benign,
'Long years have come and gone since these poor gauds were broken,
Broken and banished from a life made more divine.

'But still we keep them stored as once our sires deemed fitting,
The symbol of dark days and lives remote and strange,
Lest o'er the minds of any there should come unwitting
The thought of some new order and the lust of change.

'If any grow disturbed, we bring them gently hither,
To read the world's grim record and the sombre lore
Massed in these pitiless vaults, and they returning thither,
Bear with them quieter thoughts, and make for change no more.'

And thence I journeyed on by one broad way that bore me
Out of that waste, and as I passed by tower and town
I saw amid the limitless plain far out before me
A long low mountain, blue as beryl, and its crown

Was capped by marble roofs that shone like snow for whiteness,
Its foot was deep in gardens, and that blossoming plain
Seemed in the radiant shower of its majestic brightness
A land for gods to dwell in, free from care and pain.

And to and forth from that fair mountain like a river
Ran many a dim grey road, and on them I could see
A multitude of stately forms that seemed for ever
Going and coming in bright bands; and near to me

Was one that in his journey seemed to dream and linger,
Walking at whiles with kingly step, then standing still,
And him I met and asked him, pointing with my finger,
The meaning of the palace and the lofty hill.

Whereto the dreamer: 'Art thou of this land, my brother,
And knowest not the mountain and its crest of walls,
Where dwells the priestless worship of the all-wise mother?
That is the hill of Pallas; those her marble halls!

'There dwell the lords of knowledge and of thought increasing,
And they whom insight and the gleams of song uplift;
And thence as by a hundred conduits flows unceasing
The spring of power and beauty, an eternal gift.'

Still I passed on until I reached at length, not knowing
Whither the tangled and diverging paths might lead,
A land of baser men, whose coming and whose going
Were urged by fear, and hunger, and the curse of greed.

I saw the proud and fortunate go by me, faring
In fatness and fine robes, the poor oppressed and slow,
The faces of bowed men, and piteous women bearing
The burden of perpetual sorrow and the stamp of woe.

And tides of deep solicitude and wondering pity
Possessed me, and with eager and uplifted hands
I drew the crowd about me in a mighty city,
And taught the message of those other kindlier lands.

I preached the rule of Faith and brotherly Communion,
    The law of Peace and Beauty and the death of Strife,
And painted in great words the horror of disunion,
    The vainness of self-worship, and the waste of life.

I preached, but fruitlessly; the powerful from their stations
    Rebuked me as an anarch,* envious and bad,
And they that served them with lean hands and bitter patience
    Smiled only out of hollow orbs, and deemed me mad.

And still I preached, and wrought, and still I bore my message,
    For well I knew that on and upward without cease
The spirit works for ever, and by Faith and Presage*
    That somehow yet the end of human life is Peace.

A THUNDERSTORM

A moment the wild swallows like a flight
Of withered gust-caught leaves, serenely high,
Toss in the windrack* up the muttering sky.
The leaves hang still. Above the weird twilight,
The hurrying centres of the storm unite,
And spreading with huge trunk and rolling fringe,
Each wheeled upon its own tremendous hinge,
Tower darkening on. And now from heaven's height,
With the long roar of elm-trees swept and swayed,
And pelted waters, on the vanished plain
Plunges the blast. Behind the wild white flash
That splits abroad the pealing thunder-crash,
Over bleared fields and gardens disarrayed,
Column on column comes the drenching rain.

THE CITY

Canst thou not rest, O city,
  That liest so wide and fair;
Shall never an hour bring pity,
  Nor end be found for care?

Thy walls are high in heaven,
  Thy streets are gay and wide,
Beneath thy towers at even
  The dreamy waters glide.

Thou art fair as the hills at morning,
  And the sunshine loveth thee,
But its light is a gloom of warning
  On a soul no longer free.

The curses of gold are about thee,
  And thy sorrow deepeneth still;
One madness within and without thee,
  One battle blind and shrill.

I see the crowds for ever
  Go by with hurrying feet;
Through doors that darken never
  I hear the engines beat.

Through days and nights that follow
  The hidden mill-wheel strains;
In the midnight's windy hollow
  I hear the roar of trains.

And still the day fulfilleth,
    And still the night goes round,
And the guest-hall boometh and shrilleth,
    With the dance's mocking sound.

In chambers of gold elysian,*
    The cymbals clash and clang,
But the days are gone like a vision
    When the people wrought and sang.

And toil hath fear for neighbour,
    Where singing lips are dumb,
And life is one long labour,
    Till death or freedom come.

Ah! the crowds that for ever are flowing —
    They neither laugh nor weep —
I see them coming and going,
    Like things that move in sleep.

Grey sires and burdened brothers,
    The old, the young, the fair,
Wan cheeks of pallid mothers,
    And the girls with golden hair.

Care sits in many a fashion,
    Grown grey on many a head,
And lips are turned to ashen
    Whose years have right to red.

Canst thou not rest, O city,
    That liest so wide, so fair;
Shall never an hour bring pity,
    Nor end be found for care?

AN ODE
TO THE HILLS

'I will lift mine eyes unto the hills, from whence cometh my help.' — PSALM CXXI. I. *

Aeons ago ye were,
Before the struggling changeful race of man
Wrought into being, ere the tragic stir
Of human toil and deep desire began:
So shall ye still remain,
Lords of an elder and immutable race,
When many a broad metropolis of the plain,
Or thronging port by some renownèd shore,
Is sunk in nameless ruin, and its place
Recalled no more.

Empires have come and gone,
And glorious cities fallen in their prime;
Divine, far-echoing, names once writ in stone
Have vanished in the dust and void of time;
But ye, firm-set, secure,
Like Treasure in the hardness of God's palm
Are yet the same for ever; ye endure
By virtue of an old slow-ripening word,
In your grey majesty and sovereign calm,
Untouched, unstirred.

Tempest and thunderstroke,
With whirlwinds dipped in midnight at the core,
Have torn strange furrows through your forest cloak,
And made your hollow gorges clash and roar,

And scarred your brows in vain.
Around your barren heads and granite steeps
Tempestuous grey battalions of the rain
Charge and recharge, across the plateaued floors,
Drenching the serried pines; and the hail sweeps
Your pitiless scaurs.*

The long midsummer heat
Chars the thin leafage of your rocks in fire:
Autumn with windy robe and ruinous feet
On your wide forests wreaks his fell desire,
Heaping in barbarous wreck
The treasure of your sweet and prosperous days;
And lastly the grim tyrant, at whose beck
Channels are turned to stone and tempests wheel,
On brow and breast and shining shoulder lays
His hand of steel.

And yet not harsh alone,
Nor wild, nor bitter are your destinies,
O fair and sweet, for all your heart of stone,
Who gather beauty round your Titan* knees,
As the lens gathers light.
The dawn gleams rosy on your splendid brows,
The sun at noonday folds you in his might,
And swathes your forehead at his going down,
Last leaving, where he first in pride bestows,
His golden crown.

In unregarded glooms,
Where hardly shall a human footstep pass,
Myriads of ferns and soft maianthemums,
Or lily-breathing slender pyrolas
Distil their hearts for you.
Far in your pine-clad fastnesses ye keep
Coverts the lonely thrush shall wander through,
With echoes that seem ever to recede,
Touching from pine to pine, from steep to steep,
His ghostly reed.

The fierce things of the wild
Find food and shelter in your tenantless rocks,
The eagle on whose wings the dawn hath smiled,
The loon, the wild-cat, and the bright-eyed fox;
For far away indeed
Are all the ominous noises of mankind,
The slaughterer's malice and the trader's greed:
Your rugged haunts endure no slavery:
No treacherous hand is there to crush or bind,
But all are free.

Therefore out of the stir
Of cities and the ever-thickening press
The poet and the worn philosopher
To your bare peaks and radiant loneliness
Escape, and breathe once more
The wind of the Eternal: that clear mood,
Which Nature and the elder ages bore,
Lends them new courage and a second prime,
At rest upon the cool infinitude
Of Space and Time.

The mists of troublous days,
The horror of fierce hands and fraudful lips,
The blindness gathered in Life's aimless ways
Fade from them, and the kind Earth-spirit strips
The bandage from their eyes,
Touches their hearts and bids them feel and see;
Beauty and Knowledge with that rare apprise
Pour over them from some divine abode,
Falling as in a flood of memory,
The bliss of God.

I too perchance some day,
When Love and Life have fallen far apart,
Shall slip the yoke and seek your upward way
And make my dwelling in your changeless heart;

And make my dwelling in your changeless heart;
And there in some quiet glade,
Some virgin plot of turf, some innermost dell,
Pure with cool water and inviolate shade,
I'll build a blameless altar to the dear
And kindly gods who guard your haunts so well
From hurt or fear.

There I will dream day-long,
And honour them in many sacred ways,
With hushèd melody and uttered song,
And golden meditation and with praise.
I'll touch them with a prayer,
To clothe my spirit as your might is clad
With all things bountiful, divine, and fair,
Yet inwardly to make me hard and true,
Wide-seeing, passionless, immutably glad,
And strong like you.

INDIAN SUMMER

The old grey year is near his term in sooth,
And now with backward eye and soft-laid palm
Awakens to a golden dream of youth,
A second childhood lovely and most calm,
And the smooth hour about his misty head
An awning of enchanted splendour weaves,
Of maples, amber, purple and rose-red,
And droop-limbed elms down-dropping golden leaves.
With still half-fallen lids he sits and dreams
Far in a hollow of the sunlit wood,
Lulled by the murmur of thin-threading streams,
Nor sees the polar armies overflood
The darkening barriers of the hills, nor hears
The north-wind ringing with a thousand spears.

GOOD SPEECH

Think not, because thine inmost heart means well,
Thou hast the freedom of rude speech: sweet words
Are like the voices of returning birds
Filling the soul with summer, or a bell
That calls the weary and the sick to prayer.
Even as thy thought, so let thy speech be fair.

WE TOO SHALL SLEEP

Not, not for thee,
Beloved child, the burning grasp of life
Shall bruise the tender soul. The noise, and strife,
And clamour of midday thou shalt not see;
But wrapt for ever in thy quiet grave,
Too little to have known the earthly lot,
Time's clashing hosts above thine innocent head,
Wave upon wave,
Shall break, or pass as with an army's tread,
And harm thee not.

A few short years
We of the living flesh and restless brain
Shall plumb the deeps of life and know the strain,
The fleeting gleams of joy, the fruitless tears;
And then at last when all is touched and tried,
Our own immutable night shall fall, and deep
In the same silent plot, O little friend,
Side by thy side,
In peace that changeth not, nor knoweth end,
We too shall sleep.

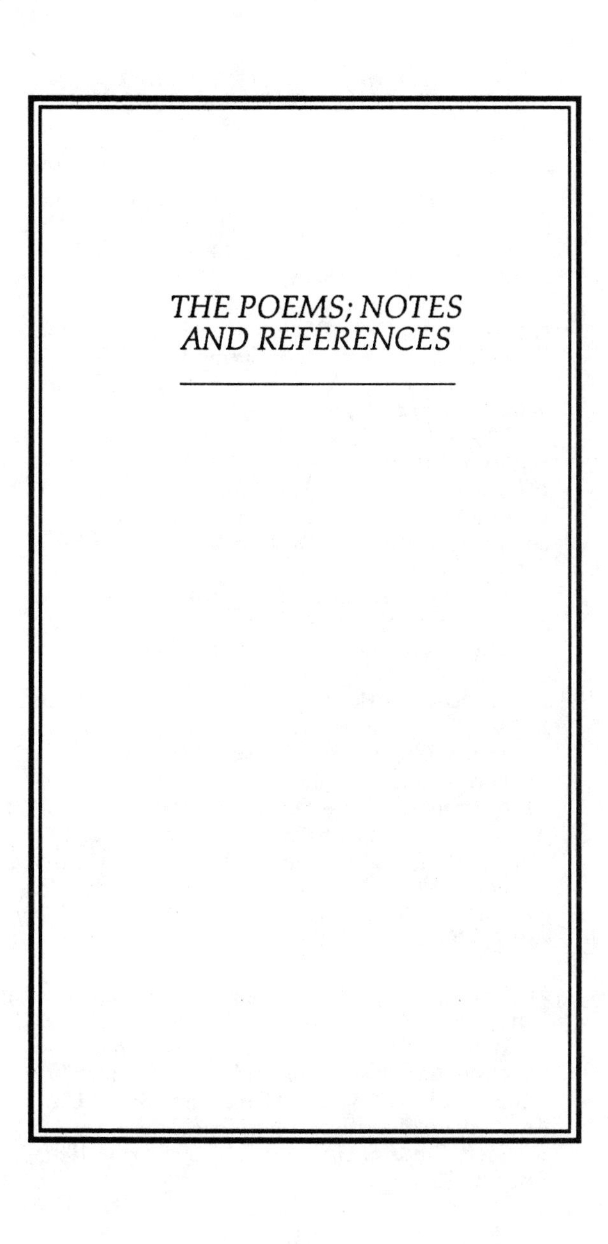

THE POEMS; NOTES AND REFERENCES

THE POEMS: NOTES AND REFERENCES

April] Connor, 162; see L.McLeod ``Canadian Post-Romanticism: The Context of Late Nineteenth-Century Canadian Poetry'' *Canadian Poetry* 14:1-37 Spring/ Summer 1984; Early, 52, 54, 55, 63.

The Frogs] see Sandra Djwa, ``Lampman's Fleeting Vision'' *Canadian Literature* 56:22-39 Spring 1973; C.F. Klinck, ``The Frogs: An Exercise in Reading Lampman'' in McMullen, 29-37; B. Davies, ``Lampman Could Tell his Frog from his Toad: A Note on Art Versus Nature'' *Studies in Canadian Literature* 2:1:129-130 Winter, 1977; D.M.R. Bentley, ``Watchful Dream and Sweet Unrest: An Essay on the Vision of Archibald Lampman'' *Studies in Canadian Literature* 7:1:5-26, Part II, 1982; Early, 63-66.
wrapt] by which Lampman intended to mean enveloped, was changed to *rapt* meaning entranced by D.C. Scott in the 1900 text of Lampman's *Poems*.

Heat] see D. Pacey, ``A Reading of Lampman's Heat'' Culture 14:292-297 September 1953; V.Y. Haines, ``Archibald Lampman: This or That'' *Revue de l'Université d'Ottawa* 41:455-471 July/September 1971; B. Davies, ``The Forms of Nature: Some of the Philosophical and Aesthetic Bases of Lampman's Nature Poetry'' in McMullen 92; D.M.R. Bentley,``Watchful Dreams and Sweet Unrest: An Essay on the Vision of Archibald Lampman'' *Studies in Canadian Literature* 6:2:188-210, Part 1, 1981.

Among the Timothy] see S.A. Coblentz, ``Archibald Lampman: Canadian Poet of Nature'' *Arizona Quarterly* 17:4:344-351 Winter 1961; K. Mezei, ``Lampman among the Timothy'' *Canadian Poetry* 5:57-72 Fall/Winter 1979; D.M.R. Bentley, ``Watchful Dream and Sweet Unrest: An Essay on the Vision of Archibald Lampman'' *Studies in Canadian Literature* 7:1:5-26, Part II, 1982; Early, 69-75.

reaper] corrected by D.C. Scott to *mower* in the 1900 text; a reaper employed a sickle which is a short-handled implement with a serrated blade used for cutting grain stalks, while a mower used a scythe which involved a two-handed sweeping motion of a long, curving blade mounted on a wooden handle. Lampman had named the wrong agricultural tool.
unbournèd] unlimited.
cicada] an insect which lives on trees and shrubs; the male makes a sharp, buzzing sound.

Freedom] Brown, 95; R.Gustafson, ``Among the Millet´´ in Gnarowski, 151; L.Dudek,``The Significance of Lampman´´ in Gnarowski, 190; F.W. Watt, ``The Masks of Archibald Lampman´´ in Gnarowski, 208; Pacey, 136.

Morning on the Lièvres] called the ``Lievre´´ in D.C. Scott's edition of Lampman's *Poems* (1900), and appearing as the ``Lièvre´´ on present day maps, this river which flows into the Ottawa northeast of the Capital at Masson, Que., was known as the Rivière aux Lièvres as early as 1833, although it appears on maps in the 1890's as the Rivière du Lièvre(s). It is officially known as the Rivière du Lièvre. The National Film Board of Canada produced a colour film in 1961, *Morning on the Lièvre* , which was inspired by this poem.

In October] see L.Dudek, ``The Significance of Lampman´´ in Gnarowski, 189.
runes] mysteries

Winter] Early, 55.

Winter Hues Recalled] Connor, 97, 99,102, 199; Brown, 89; B. Davies, "The Forms of Nature: Some of the Philosophical and Aesthetic Bases of Lampman's Nature Poetry" in McMullen, 88; Early 56-58.

Despondency] see Ralph Gustafson, ``Among the Millet'' in Gnarowski, 144-147; Pacey, 123, 128.

Gentleness] Early, 96-97.

The Truth] Connor, 98, 100.

A Night of Storm] see F.W. Watt, `` The Masks of Archibald Lampman'' in Gnarowski, 210.
chidden] rebuked, scolded.

The Railway Station] see Raymond Knister, ``The Poetry of Archibald Lampman'' in Gnarowski, 110; L.K. MacKendrick, ``Sweet Patience and her Guest, Reality: The Sonnets of Archibald Lampman" in McMullen, 52.
bourneless] boundless.

In November] Connor, 97.

The City] Collin, 25; Connor, 78, 79; F.W. Watt, ``The Masks of Archibald Lampman'' in Gnarowski, 211-212.

Solitude] Beattie, 83.
frieze] a painted or sculptured decorative horizontal strip.

April in the Hills] Connor, 162.
veery] a North-American thrush.

Life and Nature] Early, 58-59.

After Rain] Connor, 175, 199.

Comfort of the Fields] see G. Clever, ``Lampman's Comfort of the Fields'' *Journal of Canadian Poetry* 3:2: 55-62 Winter 1981.

pièd] dappled or multi-coloured.
meres] seas, bodies of standing water.
wains] large, open horse or ox-drawn vehicles used for hauling agricultural products.
thrasher] a power-driven machine used to separate grain or other seed from the straw or husk; also one who thrashes or threshes grain.

September] Early, 52, 54-55.

An Autumn Landscape] Connor, 175.

In November] see B. Davies, "The Forms of Nature: Some of the Philosophical and Aesthetic Bases of Lampman's Nature Poetry" in McMullen, 92; L. McLeod, "Canadian Post-Romanticism: The Context of Late Nineteenth-Century Canadian Poetry" *Canadian Poetry* 14:1-37 Spring/Summer 1984.
compline] in Catholic ritual the last service of the day.

Alcyone] Brown, 115; L. Dudek, "The Significance of Lampman" in Gnarowski, 194-196; Early, 31-32.
Alcyone] the brightest star in the constellation Taurus,and named after one of the seven daughters of Atlas and Pleione known as the Pleiades, who, in Greek mythology, were the attendants of Artemis and were changed into stars by the gods when they were pursued by the amorously inclined hunter, Orion.

The City of the End of Things] Collin, 25-30; Brown, 94-95; see also, Duncan Campbell Scott, "Copy ofLetter by Duncan Campbell Scott to Ralph Gustafson" in Gnarowski, 157; John Sutherland, "Edgar Allan Poe in Canada" in Gnarowski, 159-178; Archibald Lampman to Horace Scudder, 25 May 1893, in Peter E. Greig, "A Check List of Manuscript Material in the Douglas Library Archives", *Douglas Library Notes* 16:1:13 Au tumn 1967; for a reconstruction of the text see M. Gnarow ski, "The City of the End of Things: A Note on the Text" in *The City of the End of Things*. Montreal:

The Golden Dog Press, 1972; Lynn, 109; D.M.R. Bentley,``A Thread of Memory and the Fabric of Archibald Lampman's ``City of the End of Things'' *World Literature Written in English* 21:1:86-95 Spring 1982; Early, 99-102;for analogues and possible literary echoes see John Milton(1608-1674), *Paradise Lost* (1667), Book II; Edgar Allan Poe (1809-1849), ``The City in the Sea''; James Thomson (1834-1882), ``The City of Dread ful Night'' (1874).

Tartarus] in Greek mythology, a part of the underworld where the wicked are punished for their misdeeds on earth.

Personality] see Raymond Knister, ``The Poetry of Archibald Lampman'' in Gnarowski, 109-110.

The Clearer Self] Early, 34-35.

To the Prophetic Soul] Early, 30-31.

The Land of Pallas] Connor, 86-87; Brown, 105-106; F.W. Watt, ``The Masks of Archibald Lampman'' in Gnarowski, 213-215; Early 102-105.

Pallas] in Greek mythology, variously, the name of a Titan, a giant, and of an Attic hero, and forming part of the title of the goddess Pallas Athene the daughter of Zeus.She is supposed to have killed a youthful play-mate or a giant named Pallas. The Lampman reference may very well have to do with the Arcadian hero of that name who founded the city of Pallanteion also Pallantium. Arcadia, in Greece is an inland plateau in the central district of Peloponnesus which, in classical times, was quite isolated, and was inhabited by shep - herds and hunters who led a proverbially simple and natural existence. The Arcadians built the city of Megalopolis.

eyots] islets or small islands.

wist] know.

gauds] playthings or toys.

anarch] a leader of revolt.

Presage] omen, portent or indication of the future.

A Thunderstorm] see L.K. MacKendrick, "Sweet Patience and her Guest, Reality: The Sonnets of Archibald Lampman" in McMullen, 57; Early, 49.
windrack] a broken mass of clouds blown by the wind.

The City] Collin, 25-30; Pacey, 135; Early, 98-101.
elysian] pertaining to Elysium, the dwelling place assigned in Greek mythology to the blessed after death.

An Ode to the Hills] Connor, 163; Brown, 115.
Psalm CXXI] which opens with "I will lift mine eyes unto the hills ..." also refers us to Jeremiah III, 23, which says "Truly in vain *is salvation hoped for* from the hills ...".
scaurs] scars.
Titan] in Greek mythology one of a race of giant gods.

We Too Shall Sleep] Connor, 171; Lynn, lx.

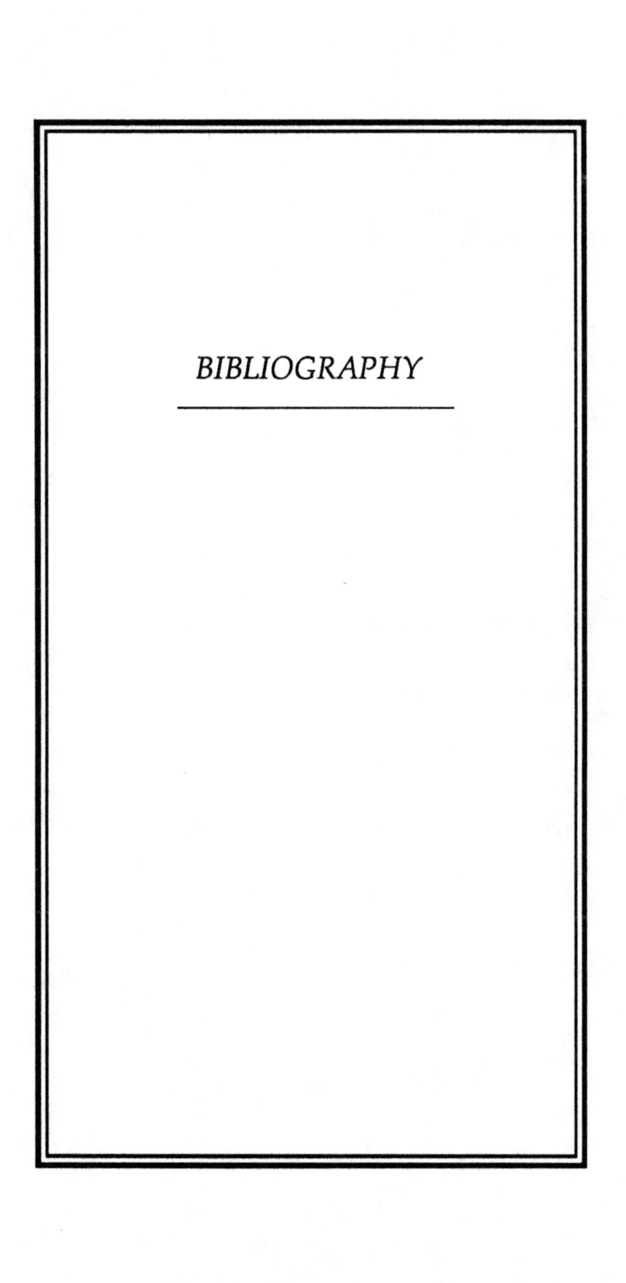

BIBLIOGRAPHY

BIBLIOGRAPHY

{ A selected list of work by, and principal material relating to, Archibald Lampman }

Work by...

AMONG THE MILLET. Ottawa: J. Durie & Son, 1888.

{ Rufus Hathaway, in his column, "The Collector" which appeared in the September 1929 number of the **CANADIAN BOOKMAN**, identified two issues of Lampman's first book.}

LYRICS OF EARTH. Boston: Copeland & Day, 1895.

{ Although the date on the title-page and in the statement of copyright appears as 1895, this book was actually published in 1896.}

ALCYONE. Ottawa: James Ogilvy, 1899.

{ A penned note by Duncan Campbell Scott on the half title page of a copy of **ALCYONE** which he had presented to Lorne Pierce in June of 1924, and which is now in the collection of Queen's University, states that when Lampman died, Scott cancelled the printing order for this book and, "...I [Scott] asked Constable to print twelve copies;...". A letter housed in the National Library of Scotland dated March 10th 1899 from T.& A. Constable, the printers, to Scott regarding this matter states, in part, "...and we make the family a present of twelve copies done up in paper covers, ...". }

THE POEMS OF ARCHIBALD LAMPMAN. Ed. with a Memoir by Duncan Campbell Scott. Toronto: Morang, 1900; Holiday Edition. 2 Vols. Toronto: Morang, 1901; Third Edition. Toronto: Morang, 1905; Fourth Edition. Toronto: Morang/ William Briggs, 1915.

LYRICS OF EARTH [:] Sonnets and Ballads. [Ed.] with an Introduction by Duncan Campbell Scott. Toronto:
Musson, 1925.

{This title has been incorrectly identified as a reprint of the 1895 **LYRICS OF EARTH** by Joe W. Kraus in his study **MESSRS. COPELAND & DAY** (Philadelphia: MacManus, 1979).}

AT THE LONG SAULT [:] And Other New Poems. [Ed.] and with a Foreword by Duncan Campbell Scott and an Introduction by E.K. Brown. Toronto: Ryerson, 1943.

SELECTED POEMS OF ARCHIBALD LAMPMAN. Chosen, and with a Memoir by Duncan Campbell Scott. Toronto: Ryerson, 1947.

THE POEMS OF ARCHIBALD LAMPMAN (INCLUDING AT THE LONG SAULT). Introduced and with a Bibliographical Note by Margaret Coulby Whitridge. Toronto: University of Toronto Press, 1974.

{ A combined reprint of the 1900 **POEMS** and of **AT THE LONG SAULT.** }

ARCHIBALD LAMPMAN: Selected Prose. Ed. with an Introduction by Barrie Davies. Ottawa: Tecumseh, 1975.

{ A selection of essays, prose fragments and some letters written by Lampman to E.W. Thomson.}

LAMPMAN'S SONNETS 1884-1899. Ed. and with an Introduction by Margaret Coulby Whitridge. Ottawa: Borealis, 1976.

ARCHIBALD LAMPMAN [:] Lyrics of Earth [.] A Working Text. Ed. and Introduced by D. M. R. Bentley. Ottawa: Tecumseh, 1978.

{ A text which restores Lampman's intended ordering of poems. }

AT THE MERMAID INN [:] Wilfred Campbell, Archibald Lampman, Duncan Campbell Scott in The Globe 1892-1893. Introduction by Barrie Davies. Toronto: University of Toronto Press, 1979.

COMFORT OF THE FIELDS. Ed. by Raymond Souster. Sutton West, Ont.: Paget Press, 1979.

{ A selection of "the best-known poems" chosen by Raymond Souster.}

AN ANNOTATED EDITION OF THE CORRESPONDENCE BETWEEN ARCHIBALD LAMPMAN AND EDWARD WILLIAM THOMSON (1890-1898). Ed. and with an Introduction by Helen Lynn. Ottawa: Tecumseh, 1980.

THE STORY OF AN AFFINITY [:] By Archibald Lampman. Edited by D.M.R. Bentley. London, Ont.: Canadian Poetry Press. 1986.

Material relating to...

Norman G. Guthrie, **THE POETRY OF ARCHIBALD LAMPMAN.** Toronto: Musson, 1927.

Carl Y. Connor, **ARCHIBALD LAMPMAN [:] Canadian Poet of Nature.** New York & Montreal: Carrier, 1929.
{Reprinted ; Ottawa: Borealis, 1977.}

Michael Gnarowski, ed., **ARCHIBALD LAMPMAN.** Toronto: Ryerson, 1970.

L. McMullen, ed., **THE LAMPMAN SYMPOSIUM.** Ottawa: University of Ottawa Press, 1976.

G.R. Wicken, comp., "Archibald Lampman [:] An Annotated Bibliography" in **The Annotated Bibliography of Canada's Major Authors [:] Volume Two.** Ed., by Robert Lecker and Jack David. Toronto: ECW Press, 1980.

L.R. Early , **ARCHIBALD LAMPMAN (1861-1899)**
{An undated and unpaginated off-print of L.R. Early's essay on Lampman in **Canadian Writers and their Works: Poetry Series. Volume Two.** Ed. by R. Lecker, J. David, E. Quigley. Intro. By G. Woodcock. Downsview (Ont.): ECW Press, 1983. pp.[134]-185.}

R.L. McDougall, ed. **THE POET AND THE CRITIC: A Literary Correspondence Between D.C Scott and E.K. Brown.** Ottawa: Carleton University Press, 1983.
(A particularly useful and revealing correspondence throwing much light, in retrospect, on Lampman and his times.)

L.R. Early, " A Chronology of Lampman's Poems" *Canadian Poetry : Studies/ Documents/ Reviews* 14 (Spring / Summer 1984) , 75-87.

L.R., Early **ARCHIBALD LAMPMAN.** Boston: Twayne, 1986
. (An important contemporary study of Lampman.)